THREE YEARS ON FIRE

ALSO BY ANDREY KURKOV
IN ENGLISH TRANSLATION

Death and the Penguin
The Case of the General's Thumb
Penguin Lost
A Matter of Death and Life
The President's Last Love
The Good Angel of Death
The Milkman in the Night
The Gardener from Ochakov
Ukraine Diaries: Dispatches from Kiev
The Bickford Fuse
Grey Bees
Diary of an Invasion
Jimi Hendrix Live in Lviv
The Silver Bone
The Stolen Heart
Our Daily War

Andrey Kurkov

THREE YEARS ON FIRE

OPEN BORDERS PRESS
LONDON

First published in Great Britain in 2025 by
Open Borders Press
an imprint of
Orenda Books
London
www.openborderspress.co.uk

9 8 7 6 5 4 3 2 1

© 2025, Andrey Kurkov

The moral right of Andrey Kurkov to be recognised as the author of this work has been asserted in accordance with the Copyright, Designs and Patents Act, 1988

All rights reserved. No part of this publication may be reproduced, stored in any retrieval system, or transmitted in any form or by any means, electronically, mechanical, photocopying, recording or otherwise, without the prior permission of the copyright owners and the publishers

A CIP catalogue record for this book is available
from the British Library

ISBN (HB) 978-1-916788-79-4

The publisher acknowledges with gratitude the editorial contribution to this text of Elizabeth Kurkov

The publisher acknowledges the original use of the author's texts in *A.B.C.* (Spain), the *Guardian*, the *Kyiv Post*, *P.E.N. International*, the *Spectator* and *The Sunday Times*.

Map © Emily Faccini

Designed and typeset in Sabon by Libanus Press Ltd
Printed and bound in Great Britain by CPI Group (UK) Ltd,
Croydon, CR0 4YY

CONTENTS

	Map	6
03.04.2024	Dummies, Drones and Gambling	9
16.04.2024	Escalation	15
23.04.2024	Ukrainian Bananas – a Story of Survival	19
30.04.2024	Stories that Come to an End	23
13.05.2024	The Circus at War	29
27.05.2024	Beautiful Views and Ugly Occupation	35
12.06.2024	Tears at the Train Station	41
24.06.2024	Generating Electricity and Crime	45
08.07.2024	War Invades the Summer	50
30.07.2024	Tuareg Rock – A Distraction from Everything Else	55
13.08.2024	Return to Kursk	61
23.08.2024	Thoughts on the Eve of Independence Day	67
27.08.2024	Moths, Cockroaches and a "Nobel Prize"	69
10.09.2024	Counting on Our Military Engineers	75
25.09.2024	Public Desertion and Going Home to Die	81
10.10.2024	War and the Psyche	87
23.10.2024	Nuclear Dreams and Reality	92
07.11.2024	Adding Fuel to the Fire	98
08.11.2024	After the Shocked Silence	102
18.11.2024	Putin and the Full Moon	105
19.11.2024	One Thousand Days	111
04.12.2024	Feeling Our Way to the End of the Year	112
17.12.2024	Naive Art and Sobering Reality	118
31.12.2024	Hope	123
01.01.2025	Fast away the Old Year Passes . . .	129
06.01.2025	Two Empty Seats	135
19.01.2025	The Dnipro at War	140
28.01.2025	A Tale of Two Machos	147
15.02.2025	On a Wing and a Prayer	153
17.02.2025	Love in the Time of Trump	156
20.02.2025	Remembering	162
21.02.2025	Still Playing Russian Roulette	164
24.02.2025	Three Years on Fire	167
28.02.2025	The White House Reality Show	172
13.03.2025	War and Europe	177
19.03.2025	Non-Essential Goods	180
29.03.2025	Thinking about the Future	186
04.04.2025	What Is in the Pipeline?	189
	So Much Left Unwritten – Epilogue	195
02.09.2025	Afterword: The "Ukraine Factor"	199
	Acknowledgements	202
	Index	205

03.04.2024

Dummies, Drones and Gambling

Advertising for online casinos has become ever more prevalent on Telegram channels which broadcast news from the front. Sometimes these adverts include reports about how much money the casino company has donated to the Ukrainian army for the purchase of drones. The mention of these donations dulls my sensitivity to the dangers of gambling. Drones are essential at the front. In his video message to the country last Monday, President Zelensky confidently declared that "Ukrainian drones will ensure our victory!" And on Tuesday, a flock of them attacked a drone factory and an oil refinery in Tatarstan, 1,200 kilometres beyond the front line.

All day and all night the buzz of drones can be heard along the 1,000 kilometres of the front line. The noise does not come from attack drones that hunt for enemy equipment and manpower but from reconnaissance drones that monitor activity and "report" on changes. For both Ukrainians and Russians, it is almost impossible to do anything on or near the front line without being noticed. Only underground activity can go unobserved, as was the case in Avdiivka, where Russian special forces quietly made their way into the city's industrial zone through tunnels. The turnover of combat drones is very high for both sides and drone production is the fastest-growing segment in both countries' economies.

One of the front lines is located in Kherson region on the eastern bank of the Dnipro River – an area mostly occupied by Russian forces. Near the flattened village of Krynki, the Ukrainian military has been controlling several square kilometres of territory along the river for many months. The width of the Dnipro at this point reaches 800 metres, making the supply of ammunition to the eastern bank hugely difficult and risky. Delivery of heavier equipment or artillery is almost impossible. This front is preserved mainly thanks to drones, which can be launched from the western bank of the Dnipro.

The village of Krynki and its surroundings are notorious among Russian soldiers. Hundreds of them have died there, and burnt-out shells of Russian tanks and armoured personnel carriers stand abandoned on the forest roads around the village. Nonetheless, Russian officers regularly order unequipped soldiers to attack. For the Russian Command, it is more important to economise on tanks and armoured personnel carriers than on soldiers. Recently, however, some surprise manoeuvres have indicated that the Russians may be seeking to reduce the loss of life. Ukrainian reconnaissance drone operators noticed a Russian truck driving at speed into the forest near Krynki. Two dozen mannequins – the kind used for shop displays – were unloaded from the truck which immediately drove away, leaving the naked mannequins on the ground.

This would seem to be the beginning of an unusual military operation. Next, most likely at night, Russian soldiers will arrive with uniforms in which to dress the dummies so that they can be placed in the trenches, in the hope that the Ukrainian military will waste time and resources engaging the dummies in battle, while groups of live Russian soldiers try to attack from some other quarter.

Tricks of this sort are commonplace. Ukrainian volunteers occasionally announce that they need mannequins for the front. But the Ukrainian forces prefer models of guns, rocket launchers and other military equipment. Mock-ups of Patriot systems or tanks – sometimes inflatable and sometimes made of lightweight materials – are being produced by several private enterprises at the request of the Ministry of Defence. The hope is that the Russian army will use expensive attack drones or missiles against these fake targets.

Thanks to Ukrainian reconnaissance drones, the mannequins dropped from a truck in the forest near Krynki will not help the Russian army. The Ukrainians have rumbled other Russian ploys. For example, silhouettes of fighter jets painted on the tarmac of Russian airfields. Ukrainian drones quickly identified the fake jets. Drone operators were especially amused by views of Russian military helicopters parked directly on top of painted SU-26 fighters.

Russia will continue to paint jets on tarmac because they do not have enough air defence systems to protect all their facilities, including airfields and refineries. Most of their air defence systems are protecting Moscow.

The Ukrainian Command is facing a very different kind of problem, which is being discussed around Ukrainian kitchen tables. Pavlo Petrichenko, a sergeant from the 59th Brigade, has created a petition on the website of the Office of the President asking for the introduction of limits on the operation of online casinos. The petition immediately collected 26,000 signatures – one thousand more than is required to ensure presidential attention. Petrichenko and many other soldiers and their families are waiting to see how the Office of the President will react to their concerns.

Petrichenko sees online gambling as a serious threat to Ukrainian society and especially to the military. In the text accompanying his petition, he writes: "For the third year running, military personnel have been away from their families, under conditions of constant stress and without opportunities for proper rest. This means they are psychologically very vulnerable. For many of them, gambling becomes the only way to deal with stress."

There have already been cases where game-addicted soldiers have spent all their money and started taking out microloans with high rates of interest. Then, to pay off their debts, they have tried to pawn military equipment, even drones or thermal imagers.

"The online gambling business directs its advertising at military personnel, using the symbols of the Ukrainian army and 'whitewashing' its activities with small charitable donations to the army," Petrichenko notes.

Not all military personnel see online gambling as a serious problem. Serviceman and blogger Maxim Skubenko believes that the danger is exaggerated. He says: "Here we have a group of capable adults whose incomes have suddenly significantly increased, and they do not know what to spend the money on. If that money goes to a legal casino, then what business is it of yours?" He does, however, suggest that financial literacy courses for military personnel could be useful.

Petrichenko, meanwhile, is relying on the Office of the

President, hoping it will prepare a bill which will ban gambling during martial law, prohibit access to online casinos for military personnel and forbid the use of Ukrainian military symbols in advertising for gambling. He also asks, among other things, for a ban on collaboration between charitable organisations and businesses involved in gambling, and a law preventing pawn shops from accepting military or dual-use items as collateral.

Gambling was banned in Ukraine in 2009, but in 2021 it was legalised again, and quickly gained popularity. There have been occasional accusations in the press against the companies operating online and offline casinos, suggesting that their ultimate beneficiaries may be Russian citizens. The lack of transparency in its structure and business operations meant that Cosmolot – the largest online casino operator in Ukraine – was granted a licence only after five attempts.

In the text accompanying his petition, Sergent Petrichenko notes that soldiers who become addicted to gambling and who fall into debt may turn out to be "useful material" for Russian military intelligence. Trying to control gambling on the front line, however, could give rise to serious conflicts within Ukrainian military units. Will commanders dare to take away soldiers' mobile phones?

Recently Kyiv's New Time radio station devoted an entire programme to this issue. I was driving into Kyiv at the time and was able to listen to it from beginning to end. I was pleased to hear the radio journalist taking this problem seriously, but the programme was interrupted twice for commercials. Both times there were adverts for *Gambler* magazine in which: "Readers can find a lot of useful information and advice!" These adverts seemed to be mocking the thoughts expressed in a radio show dedicated to the problems surrounding gambling trends in wartime. The fact is that casinos can pay more for advertising than other businesses, and it appears that media channels lack the financial or moral strength to refuse such earnings. In western Ukraine, the gaming industry has gone even further. It sponsors regular programmes on local radio which are dedicated to gaming. The purpose of the radio shows is to attract even more customers to online casinos and offline gaming spaces.

It is not yet clear who will win in this secondary "war" – the gambling industry or the anti-gambling groups among Ukraine's civilian and military population. President Zelensky has not responded to the petition so far, but he will have to. In the meantime, on popular Telegram channels, adverts for "patriotic" online casinos continue to appear between news broadcasts from the front. As the military situation becomes increasingly heated, you would think that gamers in military uniform would not have time to put down their machine guns and pick up their smartphones. But what if gaming is the only relief for soldiers in their rare moments of respite between battles? Solving this problem may prove to be more challenging than identifying fake Russian soldiers and fighter jets.

16.04.2024

Escalation

The world breathed a sigh of relief at N.A.T.O.'s response to Iran's recent attack on Israel. Ukraine sighed too, only more in envy at the thought of U.S. and U.K. aircraft shooting down Iranian drones. Almost all the missiles launched from Iran were intercepted. "If they had helped us like that, we would have liberated our occupied territories long ago!" Ukrainians wrote on social networks. "That's what 'a closed sky' means!" While American and British planes were shooting down Iranian drones over Jordan and Israel, Ukrainian mobile units in jeeps with light anti-aircraft systems were scrambling to shoot down Iranian drones launched by Russia over Ukraine.

Even President Zelensky spoke resentfully about the successful repulsion of the Iranian attack on Israel. In response, British representatives explained that Ukraine does not receive such assistance "so as not to provoke an escalation" in the war with Russia, prompting hysterical laughter from Ukrainians.

Russian troops are slowly advancing along the entire eastern front. In Donbas, they have been ordered to take the city of Chasiv Yar by May 9 – the day Russia celebrates the victory over Nazi Germany. Ukrainian military journalists write as if the city's fate was already sealed and discuss how its occupation will affect developments on the eastern front.

The costly but effective defence of Israel was undertaken to prevent an escalation in the conflict between Israel and Iran. If an Iranian missile had hit an Israeli hospital or residential building, Israel would have responded much more vigorously, and further exchanges of blows would have been very difficult to stop. An escalation in that arena would have negatively affected Ukraine, not only because the military aid that the country is counting on may have been redirected to Israel but also because an Israel–Iran war would sap the world's attention, pushing Ukraine's struggle further into the shadows.

So, Biden's efforts to keep the lid on the conflict in the Middle East are very important for Ukraine, even if we feel glum about the situation. There is, however, one piece of good news for Ukrainians in all this: according to American military experts, up to 50 per cent. of the Iranian missiles which were prepared for the attack on Israel fell out of the sky before reaching Israel or did not take off at all due to manufacturing defects. This brings into question Iran's military potential, although the Iranian drones that Russia is using against Ukraine are technically advanced and are certainly causing a lot of damage.

*

In Kyiv, meanwhile, the war between adherents of the Orthodox Church of the Moscow Patriarchate and defenders of the city's historical sites has entered a new phase. While the pro-Russian President Viktor Yanukovych was in power, the Moscow Patriarchate illegally built a church next to the site of one of Kyiv's earliest churches – Desyatynna, or the Tithe Church. The State Museum of History is nearby and has responsibility for the surrounding area, which is protected as a historical site.

A court decision was made to demolish the illegally constructed building a long time ago, but the "church" continues to function, holding regular services and broadcasting liturgical music on Saturday evenings and Sundays. Activists recently asked the management of the museum to explain why the church was still there. The museum's director replied that only the State Executive Services could deal with the question of the building's demolition, and, because of the war, these Executive Services had no money allocated for such purposes.

The activists found out how much the dismantling work would cost and set about raising the funds on social networks. In just one day they collected more than was needed. Then a construction company offered to dismantle the building free of charge so that all the money collected could be donated to the Ukrainian army. This news did not, however, please the museum's management, which seems to fear any kind of scandal. There is a tense pause as all parties await word from the State Executive Services, without whose formal permission nothing can be done.

Meanwhile, the state authorities have announced that they are preparing to check the legality of 73 Kyiv churches and their land plots which are affiliated to the Moscow Patriarchate. Each church is a separate legal entity, so 73 independent investigations will have to be carried out. That could take a very long time.

One of the reasons for the Ukrainian authorities' caution regarding the actions of the Moscow Patriarchate, even when those actions are clearly illegal, is that the church's leadership has hired a well-known American lawyer, Robert Amsterdam, to defend their interests. Amsterdam has launched a campaign in the United States in support of the Church of the Moscow Patriarchate and regularly accuses the Ukrainian leadership of persecuting believers and restricting religious freedom. This topic is readily picked up by some Republicans in America, and the Ukrainian leadership does not want to give them reasons for any anti-Ukrainian narrative, especially in the run-up to the presidential election.

Recently, in Noginsk, about 70 kilometres east of Moscow, the Russian authorities bulldozed the only Ukrainian Orthodox church in the Russian Federation. That church was built legally and had all the necessary documents to allow it to function. It seems that the American lawyer, Amsterdam, did not notice its demolition. True, nothing has been said about it in Ukraine either.

23.04.2024

Ukrainian Bananas – a Story of Survival

Spring is seeing a few positive developments away from the front. Some well-known brands have recently reopened their shops in the capital and elsewhere. Kyiv residents are especially happy about the return of Zara. McDonald's restaurants are reappearing in the south and east of Ukraine, and, at the Khmelnitsky nuclear power plant, preparatory work has begun for the construction of two new nuclear units – the fifth and sixth. With the ongoing mass destruction of Ukrainian power plants by the Russians, the country will soon face a catastrophic energy-supply situation. The new nuclear units will not be up and running any time soon but, so long as we do not allow ourselves to think about attacks on these installations, it is comforting to know that such construction plans are going ahead.

The Zaporizhzhia nuclear power plant, captured by the Russian army in March 2022, is completely shut down and the area is used by the Russians as storage space for weapons and, of course, as a tool for blackmailing the whole world.

Russia recently stepped up its attacks from Belgorod, close to the Ukrainian border. Rocket launchers in the town stand between high-rise, residential buildings. Not surprisingly, Ukrainian attack drones fly there from time to time. The explosions are loud, and the residents of Belgorod are justifiably afraid of them. Many have gone to stay with relatives in other regions of Russia, while those who decided to join the "official evacuation" have found themselves in rather remote areas of Siberia and the Urals and, according to comments on Russian social media, without the state financial support they were promised.

Those who have remained in Belgorod are watching as the city prepares for the summer. Near recreation areas and river beaches, the city authorities are installing concrete bomb shelters where people can hide when Ukrainian drones approach. Children's bulletproof vests with hoods have appeared on sale. This body armour is not cheap. Prices start at $400, but the Russian government has not offered to provide free body armour for those who live near the Ukrainian border and who regularly complain about the shelling of their town. Russia's chief television propagandist, Vladimir Solovyov, called the residents who complain "alarmist creatures".

In Ukraine, in spite of the death of hundreds of children, children's bulletproof vests have not appeared on sale. Children see and hear the sounds of war every day, and yet, on Friday mornings, many families discuss plans for the weekend, hoping there will not be an air raid. A new tourist attraction for Kyiv residents has recently appeared in the village of Rozhny, 20 minutes by road from Kyiv's northeastern limits. There you can visit two large greenhouses – one subtropical, the other tropical. Both are full of exotic plants and trees. As well as admiring the fruit-bearing orange, lemon, papaya, kumquat and mango trees, visitors can buy three new varieties of banana tree which have been bred over the last 25 years in Rozhny by Anatoly Potiy, the owner of this tropical fruit farm.

Although only an amateur horticulturalist, Potiy has made it possible for Ukrainians to grow bananas in their own homes. He has developed a miniature banana palm that grows up to 75 centimetres, a medium-sized tree that grows up to one and a half metres and a larger one that reaches two and a half metres. All three varieties allow you to grow bananas in your home. Fruit-bearing pineapple and dwarf fig trees for indoor planting are also on sale. The number of people wanting to visit his greenhouse and buy saplings has forced Potiy and his wife Tetyana to create an electronic registration system.

Potiy conducts fascinating tours of his huge greenhouses and their contents, but he does not usually explain how, during a shelling attack at the very beginning of the war, part of a neighbour's property collapsed and all the windows in his house were blown out, forcing Potiy and his wife to move into the greenhouses. They lived there for several weeks during the winter. There was no gas or electricity, and Potiy was afraid that his exotic plants would freeze. Unable to bear the constant shelling, Potiy and his wife eventually evacuated to Germany. They spent six months there while a nephew remained in Rozhny looking after the greenhouses as best he could. When Potiy returned, he found to his surprise that not a single tree or bush had died. All the trees had withstood the cold and frequent lack of water.

Russian troops never reached Rozhny. Ukrainian defence units stopped the enemy advance 30 kilometres away from the village and, thanks to this dramatic story, Potiy discovered that the varieties of banana palm and other trees that he had bred are frost-resistant and not afraid of sudden climatic changes. You could say that the astonishing survival of these trees mirrors the unexpected staunchness with which Ukrainians are facing adversity. They could not have anticipated that they would find in themselves what it takes to survive in a country under constant attack from a vicious and powerful neighbour.

30.04.24

Stories that Come to an End

Every story, even one that seems to have reached its finale, has its continuation.

Pavlo Petrichenko, the soldier of the 59th Brigade who, on March 29 of this year, created a petition to ban online casinos, died in battle on April 15. On April 16, President Zelensky promised to consider his petition and establish some kind of control over online casinos.

A new petition has appeared on the website of the Office of the President, asking that Sergeant Petrichenko be awarded posthumously the title "Hero of Ukraine". It has already received the necessary 25,000 signatures of support.

*

At the beginning of the full-scale war, Ukrainians were captivated by the heroism of the military pilot Stepan Tarabalka, known as the "Ghost of Kyiv". During the first two weeks of the war, while defending the skies over the Ukrainian capital, he shot down a good many Russian fighter jets. Tarabalka died, however, on March 13, 2022, in an unequal air battle over Zhytomyr region. No petition to the Office of the President was required to spur the authorities into granting him posthumously the title "Hero of Ukraine".

Tarabalka has become the hero of a comic book story and

is still remembered with gratitude by all Ukrainians. Recently, his mother, Natalya Tarabalka, joined the Military Chaplains Corps. "My decision to join the corps was prompted by my own spiritual experience and now I have received the necessary knowledge base for chaplaincy, I want to be needed and useful to active soldiers and veterans as well as to my family," she said.

More than two years have passed since the death of her son. During that time Natalya has created the "Warmth of a Winged Soul" health and rehabilitation centre for military personnel. She achieved this using the compensation money which she received after her son's death and with help from volunteers and local authorities whose support, she says, remains constant.

During this war, we have often heard how, instead of children continuing the work of their parents, it is parents and other loved ones who continue the work of their deceased children, husbands and wives. But sometimes there is inevitably no continuation, only a dark full stop.

At the beginning of spring, the Kvilinsky Garden, a flower farm and garden centre, founded many years ago by Jan and Olga Kvilinsky in Poltava region, ceased to exist. Jan was known for his love of roses; the varieties which he cultivated can be found in gardens all over Poltava region and beyond. As well as roses, he loved boxing and foreign languages. At the beginning of the war, Jan sent his wife and young daughter to the United States and went to the front. At the end of January, he died in Avdiivka.

"The Kvilinsky Garden is no more." This message, placed by someone on Jan's Facebook page, shocked acquaintances and strangers alike. It is not known whether his wife and daughter will return to Ukraine. Recently his brothers-in-arms organised a boxing championship in his memory, while friends from the world of horticulture appealed to people who have roses from the Kvilinsky nursery to remember Jan when the flowers bloom in their gardens.

Considering how many companies and farms have been left without owners due to Russia's aggression, we might expect the number of small and medium-sized businesses in Ukraine to have slumped. The statistics tell a different story, however. In 2023, almost 315,000 private firms were registered in Ukraine – more than in any other year of the last decade. Many of these new businesses are hair and beauty salons, often created by women – displaced women who have moved to safer regions of the country.

A large number of small construction companies have also appeared. There is a logical explanation for this too: many builders and home renovation specialists have been working for years on a cash-only basis, without being registered and without paying taxes. Private-sector work for these companies has dried up as the war has pushed housebuilding and home improvements off the agenda. At the same time, there has been a boom in central and local government programmes which fund reconstruction and repair work on housing and public facilities damaged by the war. Only officially registered, taxpaying companies can submit tenders for work on these projects, and it is worth registering to gain access to this seemingly bottomless pit of construction work.

Statistics show that, since the beginning of the war, a little more than 200,000 private businesses have closed down each year – fewer than those being opened. These statistics, however, do not include private businesses that have not been closed officially but that no longer function due to the destruction of their premises or the evacuation or death of the owners. Figures for cases like this remain a mystery.

My youngest son has been trying for several days to sign up for a driving test. All the slots for tests are booked weeks in advance and almost all of the candidates are women. Many of them are the wives of men drafted into the army. They have the family car but no licence. The gradual upward trend in the number of female drivers in Ukraine, which started from almost zero in the early 1990s, has stepped up its pace.

Swings in the number of small businesses and female drivers are interesting statistics, but for most Ukrainians, the issue of greatest concern is mobilisation. This question has divided society more radically than any other. The law on mobilisation, signed by President Zelensky, officially comes into force on May 18, but some government decisions related to it are already being implemented. These include the Ministry of Foreign Affairs' order to stop offering consular services to male citizens of military age (18–60). This means that citizens in this category who live abroad can no longer receive any documents from the Ukrainian state or renew their passports. To obtain these documents, they must return to Ukraine and register with the military. If a man of "military age" returns, he will not be allowed to leave the country again.

Rumours that such a decision was being prepared had been circulating for a long time, and it had become common to see queues of men applying for new passports at Ukrainian consulates.

Even those Ukrainian men who managed to submit passport renewal documents to a consulate will be required to return to Ukraine to receive their new passports. Ukrainian passports are valid for ten years. Once they expire, the legal status of the holder who finds themselves abroad will be in question. Ukrainians living in Europe have commented angrily to local journalists. Some say that they no longer see any point in returning to Ukraine. Others explain that they have been living in Europe for many years and have no choice but to try to obtain citizenship in their country of residence.

The German government has announced that expired Ukrainian passports will not affect the status of Ukrainian refugees and that, for travel within Europe, Ukrainians with expired Ukrainian passports will be issued with "grey passports" – an identity card used by non-German citizens and stateless people. Polish authorities have made a similar statement, although they added that, if necessary, they could assist Ukraine in returning Ukrainian citizens home for further mobilisation.

The Ukrainian government has stated that, since the start of the war, about 600,000 men of military age have left Ukraine illegally. Some analysts suggest the figure is closer to one million. How many of them will agree to return to Ukraine voluntarily must be a rhetorical question.

The new Law on Mobilisation contains articles that may worry Ukrainian citizens who have not thought about leaving Ukraine, although these stipulations are typical of any country under martial law. We are talking about the right of the state to seize private vehicles – both cars and trucks, as well as buildings and housing. In spite of the war, in 2023 Ukraine's car dealers did reasonably good business. That success is unlikely to be repeated this year given that, from May 18, your recently purchased vehicle could be confiscated for use by the army. Indeed, last year, along the main highway between Poland and Kyiv I often noticed trucks carrying brand-new S.U.V.s from Europe to car dealerships in Kyiv, Dnipro, Zaporizhzhia and elsewhere, but over the past couple of weeks on the same highway I have not seen a single one.

The new Law on Mobilisation may not impact the real estate market to the same extent. Prices for properties away from the fronts are reasonably stable and even on the rise. Closer to European borders prices are rising faster than elsewhere. Properties located five kilometres or less from the border are considered especially attractive because the owners have the right to be inside the frontier zones which are currently closed to everyone else in order to reduce illegal border crossings. And that brings us full circle to the issue of conscription.

13.05.2024

The Circus at War

Ukrainians have had two things on their minds in recent days: the Russian army's offensive in Kharkiv region and the performance of the Ukrainian duet in the Eurovision Song Contest. The Eurovision Song Contest is over. Ukraine took third place – end of story. The Russian army's offensive in Kharkiv region, on the other hand, continues, although Ukrainian official media is providing less information about what is happening on that front than it did about the winners and losers of Eurovision.

Last Friday evening we were having dinner with friends, Vasyl and Tetyana, and talking about our plans for the near future. At eight in the evening, Vasyl felt the need to turn on the television.

"We should catch up on what's going on in Kharkiv," he said anxiously.

We moved to the sofa and watched a B.B.C. journalist in Kharkiv explain, in some detail, the situation on the fringes of the city. The report included maps showing the latest Ukrainian villages to have been captured by Russian troops and news of the Ukrainian border town of Kupyansk – targeted daily by dozens of huge Russian bombs, yet still home to some 300 residents who have refused to leave the town, which is now little more than piles of rubble. The reporter's tone was dramatic, and his pessimism dulled our spirits. We turned off the television and returned to the table, our desire to talk about plans entirely extinguished.

While we were visiting Vasyl and Tetyana, our son Anton was attending an evening of stand-up comedy at the Golden Gate pub. He did not find much to laugh at. On a Friday night, there were only nine people in the audience and Anton could not remember any of the jokes told by the four comedians. "I don't think they were really in the mood to tell jokes, with so few people listening," he explained. "But at least the beer was good!"

New jokes and anecdotes are very hard to come by. This is alarming because Ukrainians have always valued humour. Not so long ago, to say that someone had no sense of humour would have been a serious insult. Times have changed. Insults as well as reasons for hatred have changed too.

*

Ukraine's circus employees recently came in for a barrage of vilification on social media. The vindictiveness against them reached such a pitch that the acting Minister for Culture, Rostyslav Karandieiev, was forced to speak out in defence of clowns, acrobats, animal trainers and other "big top" performers.

The wave of antagonism against circus workers may one day be held up as a classic example of the manipulation of mass consciousness, but it was sparked by the publication of a document listing professions exempt from military conscription. The list includes Members of Parliament, employees of weapons and ammunition factories, television journalists working for the "Unified" information channel – which observes the state information policy – and, somewhere near the end of the list, employees of the state circus.

Within an hour of the document's publication, several bloggers had launched ferocious attacks on social networks under the heading "Circus Workers Exempt from Mobilisation". Instantly this category of Ukrainians became society's number one internal enemy.

"I was outraged by the hate expressed around the topic of people working in the cultural and media sphere," Karandieiev exclaimed. "It shows disrespect for those who do their work honestly and efficiently, a primitive assessment of their social significance, and a primitive attitude towards the significance of culture in wartime."

He went on to explain what the State Travelling Circus does. This large, professional team spends eleven months a year touring throughout the free territory of Ukraine, including recently liberated cities and towns. They perform in hospitals, bomb shelters and other premises that would usually be unsuitable for their work. In 2023, more than 1,500 shows were performed, attended by 145,000 spectators.

The State Travelling Circus has chosen to exempt from conscription only people who do the fourteen jobs which are essential to the staging of performances. The remaining male workers can be drafted at any time and dozens of acrobats, gymnasts, animal trainers and clowns are already in the army.

At the start of the war, professional clown Mykola Bilenky was living and working in Great Britain. He returned to

Ukraine at the end of February 2022 and volunteered for the front. He has been treated for wounds and shell shock, but he is still fighting. In his free time, Bilenky watches circus acts on YouTube and follows the achievements of his two sons, who perform with a circus-on-ice troop mainly in the south and south-east of Ukraine. Before leaving for the U.K., Bilenky lived in Lviv and was responsible for the Lviv State Circus' New Year shows for children. The props for those performances, many of which he made himself, are in storage, waiting for Bilenky, after the war.

"Is a circus necessary in wartime? Certainly it is! Children are growing up, they need to relax, to see something that makes them feel happy," Bilenky says. He has already lost two close colleagues in action.

Bilenky's call sign is "Lucky Harlequin". Call signs are usually very short, one- or two-syllable words, like "North", "Devil" or "Demon". His fellow soldiers have probably shortened "Lucky Harlequin", but Bilenky considers himself lucky because he is still alive and still fighting. The work of a clown requires rigorous physical training and, at 53, in terms of physical fitness, Bilenky is better prepared for active service than many younger people.

Timur Kuliev is another acrobat and clown who has been in the Ukrainian army since the beginning of the full-scale invasion. He is 33 and grew up in a family of circus performers, taking part in his first show at the age of three. His wife is also a circus performer. Before the war, they toured in Ukraine and Europe.

"As a clown, I'll tell you this: I think I'm the funniest person in our unit. If I can convey my positive mood to others, then I do it!" he says. In the circus, he juggled sixteen-kilogram weights. At the front, he juggles apples to cheer up his fellow soldiers. "It's simply impossible to leave the circus. It's a profession that gives joy to spectators and performers alike. The circus is my drug," Kuliev says.

At the Kyiv State Circus, preparations are under way for the Forum of Amateur Circus Acts. On May 31, amateur circus artists from all over Ukraine will take part in master classes and round tables. Many of the participants will have the opportunity to display their talents in the arena of Ukraine's main circus. Then on June 1, there will be an international circus act competition.

The recent wave of hostility against circus performers is fading from social media memory, but the experience of being the target of so much anger has encouraged the Kyiv State Circus to communicate better about its work. Weekly guided tours of the circus have been introduced. They are conducted by the director, Vladislav Kornienko, and visitors attend rehearsals, meet circus performers and tour the costume- and prop-making workshops.

While circus professionals like Timur Kuliev and Mykola Bilenky are fighting at the front, foreign clowns come to Ukraine to replace them. One such, Marco Rodari (a relative of the Italian children's writer Gianni Rodari), is well known to the children of frontline towns and cities in Zaporizhzhia, Kharkiv and Donbas regions. He has visited a dozen times, organising magic shows and circus performances for children who live under the constant threat of air raids. Rodari can no longer perform in Bakhmut or Chasiv Yar. These towns have been all but wiped off the map, but the children who attended his performances there, earlier in this war, will remember the Italian clown for the rest of their lives.

Meanwhile, Russia's main circus troupe, the Moscow Circus, is performing at venues around the occupied territories. They brought their show with the worrying title "History" to Luhansk and have already given 23 performances. They have also performed in Alchevsk, Stakhanov and other occupied cities. On May 9, Soviet Victory Day (probably Russia's most important public holiday), a delegation of Russian circus performers laid flowers and wreaths at monuments to Soviet soldiers killed between 1941 and 1945. We can safely say that the Russian and Ukrainian circuses are at war, just as Ukrainian history is at war with Russian history. While the Russian circus is helping to embed the Kremlin's version of Ukrainian history in the minds of residents in occupied territories, the Ukrainian circus is defending its reputation within Ukraine from hatred on social media.

In Kharkiv, there remains little to laugh about, but life goes on. At half past five in the morning, on the city's central streets, final-year school pupils could be seen rehearsing the traditional waltz for their graduation ceremony, planned for late May.

27.05.2024

Beautiful Views and Ugly Occupation

This spring, Odesa has seen the birth of a new tradition. An increasing number of residents go down to the shore in the early morning to greet the dawn. Videos of Odesa's sunrise appear on social networks every day, often accompanied by texts carrying the message: "If you can't change anything, then enjoy every moment of beauty!" In other words: "Live for today! Tomorrow may never come!"

As the sea gets warmer, the sunrise spectators take a swim before getting started with their day. The water in the Black Sea around Odesa is considered to be reasonably clean this year. The fall in the number of ships entering the region's ports must be having a positive impact on the area's natural environment. There are also fewer Russian warships on the Black Sea. Thanks to Ukrainian naval drones, part of the Russian fleet lies on the seabed. To evade further attacks, Russia has moved most of its navy previously in Crimea to the Caspian Sea and the port of Novorossiysk on the Caucasus coast.

The ban on industrial fishing in the Ukrainian waters of the Black Sea has led to a huge increase in fish stocks. Amateurs standing on the seashore with fishing rods – a mode of fishing that is not prohibited – can catch excellent fish in large quantities and the locals are happy to buy it.

While Odesa's residents are watching the dawn seascapes,

fishing and shuddering under frequent air raid sirens and explosions, people in Lviv have been surprised to hear about an event that recently took place in their city. As you might expect in wartime, important meetings and conferences often remain unannounced until after they have taken place. That was how a two-day Forum of the Russian Opposition was organised in Lviv. The full list of participants and guests remains a mystery, but it is known that the forum was attended by volunteers from all three Russian battalions fighting on the side of the Ukrainian army.

The speeches by the Russian participants have not been published, but Mikhailo Podolyak, Adviser to the Head of the Office of the President, was one of the V.I.P. Ukrainian speakers at the event. In his address, he urged the Russian participants to "Be ready to seize power in Russia when the current regime begins to crumble!" Podolyak is convinced that this opportunity will arise at some point in the coming year and that the collapse of Putin's vertical power structure will be sudden and rapid. The forum itself was approved by General Budanov, head of the Main Intelligence Directorate of the Ministry of Defence, who said that such events bring the end of Putin's regime closer.

The only public figure known to have criticised the Forum of the Russian Opposition was the Mayor of Lviv, Andriy Sadovyi. He had been kept in the dark about the meeting and he asked Ukraine's Security Services for clarification on the event – keen to show Lviv residents that he had not been involved in preparations for the forum and had not given his consent to its being held in Lviv. For many Ukrainians, there are no "good Russians", and the forum has led to accusations against Sadovyi of collaboration with an enemy force.

Podolyak felt the need to apologise to the Russian oppositionists for Ukrainians' indiscriminate hatred of all Russians. He noted that the war had left citizens incapable of differentiating between Russian supporters of Putin's regime and opponents of it. "This is easy to understand and a normal, emotional reaction brought about by the war," he said.

Forty Russian opposition groups and organisations were represented at the forum, but no-one attended on behalf of the Anti-Corruption Foundation – the party of the late Alexei Navalny. In an interview with Ukrainian television, Ilya Ponomarev, a former member of the Russian State Duma who now lives in Ukraine, said that Navalny's party and some other Russian political émigré groups do not support the idea of an armed struggle for change in Russia and, therefore, could not take part in the forum. These Russian anti-Putin politicians are dreaming of coming to power through democratic means – through elections. I envy them their imagination.

Annexed Crimea and areas of Donbas which were occupied in 2014 have long been included in the official geography of Russia for electoral purposes, while the occupied territories of Zaporizhzhia and Kherson regions recently experienced their first "Russian presidential elections". I wonder if Navalny's party is ready to conduct an election campaign in the occupied territories of Ukraine so that they can come to power in Russia by "peaceful, democratic means".

The Russian government has recently begun to pay closer attention to the issue of "reliability" among Ukrainians who chose to remain in the occupied territories. Residents who did not immediately agree to take Russian passports are suspected of being unreliable even if they later applied for one. At the same time, the Russian authorities have announced a plan to nationalise the property of Ukrainians who fled the occupied territories. Ukrainians who do not want to lose their property must urgently go to their former place of residence – in Melitopol, Genichesk, or other cities and villages captured by the Russian army – to reregister their houses, apartments and land plots according to Russian law. First, however, they must acquire a Russian passport.

If owners do not get Russian documents for themselves and their property, or if utility bills have been left unpaid for one year, the property of Ukrainian citizens will be nationalised and transferred to new owners chosen by the occupation administration. Most likely, the new owners will be immigrants from the Russian Federation.

The majority of refugees from the occupied territories have said goodbye to their houses and apartments, but some are determined to maintain their property rights. To this end, they embark on the risky journey to occupied territory. Citizens of Ukraine can only enter the Russian Federation through Moscow's Sheremetyevo Airport. This means that they must fly from Europe to Istanbul or Dubai and from there use a Russian airline to fly to Moscow.

Even if a Ukrainian citizen reaches Sheremetyevo, there is no guarantee that he or she will get through airport passport control, and, even if they pass all the checks, they may still not achieve the goal of securing their property. One former resident of Melitopol, who did not want to give his name, but let's call him Ihor, said that at least 50 Ukrainian citizens – former residents of occupied territories – flew into Moscow on the same flight as him. After long interrogations and checks, only two were allowed into Russia. Ihor was one of them.

Having reached Melitopol he immediately went to apply for a Russian passport, which he received ten days later. However, the occupation administration then refused to issue him with documents for his apartment. It turned out that the entire building in which Ihor's home is located had already been "nationalised" and earmarked for future migrants from Kazakhstan, Belarus and the Russian Federation.

The Russian government has made Melitopol the "capital" of occupied Zaporizhzhia region. The city's population is presently more than 150,000 – slightly larger than before the war. The local occupation authorities, together with the Russian Ministries of Foreign Affairs and Internal Affairs have launched a programme called "Zaporizhzhia Virgin Lands Resettlement" through which families are lured to the occupied territory with promises of high salaries and excellent social conditions. Interestingly, some fifteen years ago, this strategy was used in another resettlement programme – one aimed at developing the Far East of the Russian Federation. At that time, Russia persuaded young families from Ukraine, Belarus and other countries to resettle in the Far East, with very similar promises.

The current resettlement strategy is very targeted. "We are assessing the demand in Zaporizhzhia region for personnel with specific skills," said Yuri Guskov, temporary "Minister for the Economy" of the occupied part of the region, in an interview with Russian journalists. "We need potential business leaders and investors, and we are compiling a list of applicants who are ready to come to our territory from abroad. After checks and approvals by all the special authorities, we will move families so that they can perform specific tasks. Our goal is to integrate such families into the economy [of the region] through social programmes . . . as quickly as possible."

While Russia is openly working to change the ethnic composition of the occupied territories of Ukraine, a new pedestrian bridge has been opened in Kyiv to mark the city's 1,542nd birthday. The bridge took four years to build, including a four-month halt in the work at the beginning of the full-scale invasion. Constructed using some of the last steel produced at the now-destroyed Azovstal plant, the bridge is a monument to the Mariupol steelworks, its workforce and the men and women who died defending it. Fittingly, former residents of Mariupol were among the first people to walk across the bridge, which offers views of the Dnipro River shoreline and will, no doubt, attract people who wish to gaze at the dawn over Kyiv – curfew rules allowing.

12.06.2024

Tears at the Train Station

I often pass through the Slovak town of Kosice, 120 kilometres from the border with Ukraine. A little train, consisting of two old carriages, runs twice a day between Kosice and the Ukrainian town of Mukachevo. It is usually crowded and almost all the passengers are Ukrainian. On my most recent journey, the carriages were half-empty, but that was not what surprised me the most.

While waiting on the platform in Kosice, I noticed a young Ukrainian couple, perhaps in their mid-thirties. The woman was crying and hugging the man. Their conversation seemed nervous. "He must be returning to Ukraine to go to the military registration and enlistment office, and then he will be off to the front," I thought.

Since May 18, a new law on mobilisation obliges all men of draft age living abroad to return to Ukraine and report to the conscription office.

When the train started moving, my scenario about the couple fell to pieces. The man remained on the platform while the woman sat down in the carriage opposite me, still crying. I tried to imagine the purpose of her journey. Perhaps she was going to visit relatives. Perhaps she was going to pick up some documents for the man. One thing seemed clear: he had somehow managed to leave Ukraine and had no intention of returning to his homeland, at least not for now.

It is estimated that at least 800,000 men have fled the country since February 2022. Many more left before the war to work in Europe or elsewhere. The Law on Mobilisation obliges them all to return home. The vast majority do not intend to return and that makes them potential felons.

Ukrainian citizens who refuse to obey conscription notices are already receiving three-to-five-year prison sentences. Recently, Hryhoriy Sirets, a resident of the Lyubeshivsky district of Volyn region, was sentenced to three years in prison for refusing to join the army. He had refused on the grounds that he had to care for his elderly mother-in-law. The Kivertsi court, also in Volyn region, sentenced a 21-year-old resident to three and a half years in prison for failing to show up at the marshalling point having received a summons for military service. The Kivertsi court made this decision before the new law on mobilisation came into force, but that does not explain the harsh sentence. The bill lowered the age of those who can be mobilised from 27 to 25, but not to 21. Compulsory military service for men between the ages of 18 and 27 was on the statute books in February 2022 but was halted at the beginning of the war.

No doubt the 21-year-old's defence lawyer will file an appeal, but who knows when it will be heard? Ukraine's courts have suffered from a catastrophic shortage of judges from long before the start of the war. Currently, the judicial system lacks almost 2,500 judges. There are courts where two judges are trying to do the work of 24 and others that do not function at all.

To date, about 8,000 charges of desertion and more

than 10,000 charges of "unauthorised abandonment of the location of military service" have been added to the tens of thousands of criminal and administrative cases that have not yet been brought to court due to staffing shortages.

Eighteen thousand servicemen is the equivalent of between two and three divisions – a significant military force. Simply putting them all in prison would only weaken the front line. Perhaps it was this that guided M.P.s to propose a bill allowing soldiers who have committed desertion or another offence for the first time to avoid criminal proceedings. Instead, they may voluntarily return to their units. This remedy, however, is only possible if the commander responsible is willing to take the soldier back.

There are interesting legal issues to consider here. Leaving the country clandestinely has not been made a criminal offence. For now, it is an "administrative violation" for which anyone caught faces a fine. A person's first attempt to evade military service is, likewise, punishable by a fine, while second and subsequent cases of evasion are criminal offences, punishable by a prison sentence.

In a post-war scenario in which large numbers of Ukrainian men decide to return home, and those who evaded conscription inside the country come out of the woodwork, the judicial system would be paralysed. But perhaps I am allowing my imagination to run away with me. Ukraine will need people to rebuild the country. An amnesty may be considered the best option.

For now, Ukraine's borders with Romania, Moldova, Slovakia, Hungary and Poland are the scene of frequent clashes between border guards and Ukrainians who are trying to escape the war. In these increasingly violent skirmishes, people on both sides have been killed or wounded.

A few nights ago, a truck with a tarpaulin-covered trailer and Ministry of Defence licence plates crossed the Ukrainian border into Hungary. In the morning, the vehicle was found empty in a field. Very soon, near the village of Barabash, 32 Ukrainians who had clandestinely entered the European Union inside the truck were detained by Hungarian police.

The vehicle's number plates were false. The truck will eventually be returned to Ukraine, but most likely the men will be granted refugee status. When they have settled in Hungary or some other European country, they will gather their wives and children around them. The wives (provided they have no medical training, which would make them liable for Ukrainian military service) and the children will be able to come and go. Then, these families will occasionally need to retrieve something from their homes or visit a relative. The wife will prepare to cross the border, and the couple will stand crying on the station platform – she, because parting in wartime is always painful. He will shed tears at the thought that he may never be able to return freely to his native Ukraine.

24.06.2024

Generating Electricity and Crime

Over the last two months, Kyiv has started to sound like a tractor factory. I have never been inside one, but the noise on many of the city's streets brings to mind a heavy machinery plant and it comes from the petrol-powered generators which have come to replace mains electricity.

Every 15 to 20 metres along Yaroslaviv Val – a café-lined street near the Golden Gate – generators stand rumbling from the early morning. The noise goes on all day except, perhaps, for three or four hours in the afternoon, when mains electricity reappears and the street becomes blissfully quiet.

In the evenings, the power goes off again and the low grumble of generators fills the air. Power-cut schedules for each city district are available online, and businesses – especially bars and restaurants – are careful to ask customers using bank cards to pay before the power goes off and the time for candlelight and cash begins.

As well as increasing noise pollution, power outages have been the indirect cause of fires in apartments. Kyiv residents who can afford them buy mini-generators and power-hoarding devices that allow them to keep domestic appliances working when there is no mains electricity. People with less money must be creative and many connect car batteries to their apartment's electrical system. As soon as the power is restored to their building the first thing people do is charge everything that can be charged: their power banks, mobile phones, computers and, if they are using one for power supply, their car batteries. Several of these D.I.Y. systems have exploded while being charged, sometimes causing serious injury and damage to buildings.

At the same time, fires of a rather different nature have become a feature of night-time Kyiv. Parked cars are being set alight, and the vehicles concerned invariably belong to military personnel or military units. The pattern was soon noticed by police and security services. Their investigations led to the arrest of some unlikely culprits: thirteen- or fourteen-year-old young people. It seems that the Russian special services are offering Ukrainian teenagers "some extra money" in exchange for acts of arson. The Russian services approach teenagers whose activity on social media indicates that they may be interested in this work. First, they are offered between $100 and $300 to leave anti-Ukrainian graffiti on exterior walls. The teenagers are expected to send pictures of their handiwork to their Russian clients, who, if satisfied, then ask the young people to set fire to Ukrainian military vehicles in return for a much larger reward.

Russian handlers tell the teenagers that, even if they are caught, they are too young to be prosecuted. What the Russians do not explain is that acts of arson committed on the orders of enemy forces are classified as terrorism, and, in Ukraine, the age of criminal responsibility for acts of terrorism is fourteen.

A mother and her fourteen-year-old son were detained recently after they set fire to a serviceman's car in Kyiv. They had made the journey to the capital from Chernihiv region, especially to earn money by committing arson. The mother explained that she had accrued large debts and had no other way of paying them off.

It seems Russian special services have enough human resources to monitor the activity of Ukrainian children on social networks. I wonder whether this army of spies is divided into units according to the age group they are targeting, but I assume that influencing Ukraine's adult population remains the priority for Russia. Thousands of Russian bots are planted in Ukrainian chats dedicated to conscription and how to evade it, or when and how the war might end. The bots are there to stir up and maintain panic and, of course, to persuade men to evade conscription.

Resistance to mobilisation inside Ukraine cannot be blamed entirely on Russian interference, but the recent spike in the number of attacks on the employees of military registration and enlistment offices does indicate that outside forces are at play and that they are having an effect. Conscription office employees are attacked in the course of their official duties – for example, when delivering call-up papers to individuals – as well as on their way home from work. A targeted campaign against the conscription system has evolved, prompting Parliament to vote in a law on the establishment of a specialised military police force with the same structure as the regular police force but one that will support the employees of military registration and enlistment offices and search for draft dodgers. The officers will have more invasive powers than ordinary police, allowing them to enter private homes without a court order. They will also patrol populated areas and have the right to stop and search cars and, of course, check the documents of drivers, passengers and pedestrians.

According to the new law, the number of personnel in this new force must not exceed 1.5 per cent. of the total number of armed forces personnel. So, we are talking about a new armed force with up to 150,000 employees. I wonder where these military police will come from, especially given a recent Cabinet of Ministers' decree restricting the share of regular police officers who can be reserved from mobilisation to no more than 50 per cent.

Is the plan to send police officers to the front and send soldiers away from it to serve in the military police? The theme of conscription remains extremely divisive, but most Ukrainians understand that without more soldiers, the future is bleak. In a recent interview with the *Philadelphia Inquirer*, the head of the Intelligence Department of the armed forces, General Budanov, said: "There is no Armageddon in Ukraine at the moment, but the situation is very difficult." In his opinion, for at least another month, the Russian army will put pressure on the entire front line, trying to achieve some identifiable progress before the special anniversary (75th) N.A.T.O. summit, scheduled for mid-July.

This period of increased pressure on the front could have prompted discussion of the need to call up more regular police officers and employees of other security agencies who until recently were exempt from conscription. Criminal activity in Ukraine is not decreasing, however, and requires a strong police force.

New forms of criminal activity are appearing precisely because of wartime conditions. Last week saw the arrest of racketeers in Cherkasy. They had chosen their victims from among the families of killed servicemen. By intimidation and blackmail, a criminal gang tried to extort the compensation payment of fifteen million hryvnias (approximately £285,000) from the family of a dead soldier. In addition to demanding money, they told the family to officially recognise a member of their gang as the illegitimate son of the killed soldier, so that he could claim state financial assistance.

As Ukraine's criminal elements are developing cruel schemes to entrap new victims, Russia is paying Ukrainian youth to commit acts of treachery. Will the teenagers who are setting fire to a Ukrainian military vehicle for $500 become "professional" criminals in the future? The chances of this happening surely increase if they are not apprehended and dealt with appropriately because too many police officers and investigators have been sent to the front.

Perhaps we will not need a new force to track down draft dodgers. It may become easy enough to find them once the winter sets in. They will be in cafés and co-working spaces where generators rumble. We will all have to use them because it will be impossible to survive shut up in our dark and freezing apartments. Representatives of the national electricity generating company D.T.E.K. have announced that this winter Ukrainians will have to spend up to 20 hours a day without mains electricity.

08.07.2024

War Invades the Summer

Last weekend, for the first time since the start of the full-scale war, signs saying "No vacancies" appeared outside Odesa hotels. The city is abuzz with holidaymakers. From early morning, thousands of people flock to the beaches, and in the evenings, the restaurants, theatres and cinemas are crowded. Despite the regular shelling of the entire region, the national railway has been forced to lay on an additional Kyiv–Odesa train. For the residents of other air raid-smitten cities, Odesa's charm still outweighs the risks.

In the heatwave that has struck the country, the pull of the seaside is overwhelming, but only two of Ukraine's Black Sea coastal resort areas remain accessible: Mykolaiv and Odesa. Mykolaiv region is closer to Crimea and, therefore, more dangerous. The main targets for Russia's ballistic missiles in Odesa region are ports and military infrastructure, including air defence systems, but holidaymakers are more afraid of Russian sea mines. Some holidaymakers leave the beach for a while when they hear explosions coming from the port, but they soon return and continue to enjoy the sun, sea and sand.

Since the beginning of the war, the Carpathian Mountains have been considered a safer holiday destination than the Black Sea coast, and Odesa residents often prefer to go there for a complete break from the anxiety of daily attacks.

Russians have a choice of familiar resorts: the Black Sea coast of the Caucasus, the Azov Sea, including occupied coastal areas of Ukraine, and even the Georgian coast with its luxurious beaches. And yet many Russians stubbornly head to Crimea for their holiday, encouraged by government statements about improvements to the peninsula's resort infrastructure. Russia's second-largest budget allocation, after military expenditure, is for propaganda. It was propaganda-budget money that paid for the purchase of ten ocean sharks from Singapore which are destined to entertain holiday-makers in Crimea. The sharks are now in St Petersburg, resting before their 2,000-kilometre road journey south in special tanks filled with ocean water.

The journey will be stressful for both the sharks and the drivers. To reach the peninsula they will have to cross the bridge joining Russia to Crimea which was constructed between 2016 and 2019. Ukrainian military intelligence has promised to destroy the bridge by the end of this summer and the Russian authorities regularly close it to traffic and impose ever stricter rules for bridge users when it is open. Security guards carry out random checks on cars, forcing drivers and passengers out of their vehicles and going through every piece of luggage. The cars themselves are checked very carefully by X-ray machines. Sometimes, there is a line of 1,500 cars waiting to cross the bridge.

While Russians travelling to Crimea may be able to prepare themselves mentally for a slow journey, I doubt they fully accept the risk of being killed or wounded during their holiday. The many Russian military facilities in Crimea – often located near the shore – are legitimate targets for

Ukrainian missiles and drones. Russian air defences shoot them down right over the beaches where people are relaxing. Recently, about 150 Russian holidaymakers were injured and four people, including two children, were killed when a Ukrainian missile was brought down over a beach in Sevastopol. Among the injured was the family of Oleg Averyanov, a high-ranking Russian official from Magadan.

Why did Averyanov take his family 11,000 kilometres to holiday in Crimea when residents of Russia's Far East usually prefer China, where there are purpose-built resorts for Russians? The answer seems to be that the Russian government regularly reminds its officials that staying in Russia for their holidays is a patriotic gesture that strengthens the trust between the authorities and the people. Holidaying in annexed Crimea is doubly patriotic because it requires courage, and it can earn officials credit with the Kremlin. Crimea is also used by the Kremlin for "soft" punishment of cultural figures who want to atone for their anti-war statements or attempts to escape abroad. These malefactors are asked to tour Crimean concert venues, military units and hospitals for injured soldiers on the peninsular.

Ukrainians have been thinking more about the peninsular since the recent release, in a prisoner exchange, of Nariman Dzhelyal. He is the Deputy Chairman of the banned Crimean Tatar Parliament who was convicted on trumped-up charges and sentenced to seventeen years in prison in September 2022.

Immediately after his release, Dzhelyal's wife Leviza and their four children left Crimea, and the family was reunited in Kyiv. They have no way back. Dzhelyal cannot return to Crimea until the territory is liberated. The family might be able to sell their home there, but it is possible that the Russian authorities will decide to "nationalise" it, just as they nationalised the home of the Ukrainian Crimean Tatar singer Jamala – winner of the 2016 Eurovision Song Contest. She was convicted *in absentia* of "spreading fake news about the Russian army" and put on the wanted list. Jamala has been living in Kyiv for several years and she has removed her parents from annexed Crimea. "Now they are rummaging through my father's things," she has written in an anguished post on Facebook.

Confiscation and "nationalisation" of property belonging to Crimeans disloyal to the Russian government began in 2014. The process continues. It happened recently to a villa belonging to Sofia Rotaru – a very well-known singer from the Soviet period who has Ukrainian citizenship and who has spoken out against the Russian aggression. The new oceanarium to which the Singapore sharks will be transported from St Petersburg will be built somewhere near Rotaru's villa in Yalta. Perhaps her building will even be incorporated into the oceanarium complex.

Another planned tourist attraction for Crimea is a crocodile park in Feodosia, but despite these efforts, local authorities will have trouble attracting holidaymakers to the peninsula. The violent scenes on a Sevastopol beach prompted an unexpected wave of criticism from residents against the municipal authorities who had previously resisted building bomb shelters. The construction of 600 of them across the Sevastopol area has been given the go-ahead. No doubt, once in place, these shelters will serve to remind residents and visitors that they are in a war zone and not in a safe Black Sea holiday resort.

As I write this, the air raid siren has sounded. I think about leaving the café where I am working and heading for a shelter, but before I can make a move, several huge explosions sound very close by, and soon enough I learn that Ukraine's central children's hospital has taken a direct hit. I am afraid there will be terrible news to come. For now, my son has gone to help clear the rubble – which is all that remains of one of the hospital's older buildings.

30.07.2024

Tuareg Rock – A Distraction from Everything Else

The hot summer continues in Kyiv, occasionally interrupted by thunderstorms and rain. This year, the heat has often come from Africa. We have seen layers of dust on our cars and in our village rainwater barrel. Meteorologists tell us it is sand brought by strong winds from the Sahara. It seems incredible that wind can carry sand across 4,000 kilometres – even more incredible than the recent attack by a Ukrainian drone on the Olenya airfield in Russia's polar north. Located inside the Arctic Circle, the airfield is 1,800 kilometres from our northern border and is favoured by the Kremlin regime for launching strategic bombers against Ukraine.

During this war, cultural phenomena have also travelled far and fast. Already on the evening of July 27, in the centre of Kyiv, by the entrance to Bar 13, a group of young people were gathered around a smartphone, listening attentively to music with obvious North African rhythms. "This is Tinariwen," explained a funky-looking young person who we assume was at least eighteen years old. "They are the coolest Tuareg group! But there is Terakaft as well. I'll find you a clip by them now."

Yes, by the evening of the day on which Tuareg forces ambushed a detachment of Wagner Group mercenaries, the musical tastes of some Ukrainian youth had already shifted. News of the ambush, which occurred in the Malian region of the Sahara Desert, on the border with Algeria, spread like wildfire and soon Ukrainian social networks were hosting discussions about the Tuareg people, their culture and their fight for independence. On Facebook, memes appeared showing a Tuareg Volkswagen surrounded by the bodies of dead Wagner Group mercenaries. At the same time, a selection of Tuareg music became widely available.

Something similar happened in early 2022 when Ukrainian troops prevented the Russian army from reaching Kyiv and forced the aggressor to flee back to Belarus. At that moment, the world suddenly became interested in all things Ukrainian.

From the comments under the Tuareg music video clips, I can see that it is not just Ukrainians who have started to follow this cultural phenomenon. Viewers from many countries express support for the Tuaregs in their fight against the visiting "musicians" – an image used in the Wagner Group's recruitment campaign. "Join our orchestra!" is one of their advertising slogans.

Representatives of the Wagner Group in Russia admitted losses in Africa, while Russian "military bloggers" have insisted that the Tuaregs' attack was supported by Ukrainian intelligence and that there were Ukrainian special forces with the Tuaregs who ambushed the Russian mercenaries. Soon after the battle, a photograph appeared on social media showing armed Tuaregs waving both their own and Ukrainian flags. This may have been simply Photoshopped, but since the Tuaregs are fighting the military dictatorship in Mali, which is being kept in place with the help of Russian mercenaries, the Tuaregs' support for Ukraine would come as no surprise.

The blaze of interest in Tuareg music here is similarly

unsurprising. Ukrainians have a tradition of appreciating foreign cultural phenomena, so long as they are not being rammed down our throats. For example, the Japanese three-line haiku has become a popular medium for Ukrainian military personnel who feel the need to write about life at the front, the war, and the state of the soul. I know some of these haiku authors and can share a few examples:

> Looking at the sunset
> Together with sunflowers
> How can we reach our positions alive?
> (by Andrii Panasiuk)

> A samurai has no goal
> But paperwork
> Cannot wait
> (by Pavlo Bilous)

> I will give a full report
> How I contemplate the cherry blossom
> No extraordinary events (on the front line)
> (by Ostap Kryvdik)

I imagine that the Japanese Minister for Education, Culture, Sport, Science and Technology, Mr Masahito Moriyama, who recently made an official visit to Kyiv, will have been told about this literary trend among Ukrainian soldiers. Japanese culture and literature were quite popular in Ukraine even during Soviet times. The Russian aggression has brought Japan and Ukraine closer. Minister Moriyama has invited Ukrainian youth to enrol in Japanese universities to study culture and language as well as technical subjects.

As the war rages on, Ukraine's youth can perhaps take some comfort in discovering new forms of music, such as Tuareg rock, and in the promises of more opportunities to study abroad, at least once the war is over. The Tuaregs' routing of the Wagner mercenaries has played another important role in Ukraine. It has distracted Ukrainians' attention from a recent high-profile political murder that briefly divided society. On July 19, very close to her home in Lviv, Professor Iryna Farion, a militant opponent of the use of the Russian language in Ukraine, was fatally wounded by a shot to the temple.

Farion's video interviews and public speeches were often used by Russian television propagandists as evidence of the presence of fascists and Nazis in Ukraine. Farion was fired from her post at Lviv State University for insisting that Russian-speaking soldiers in the Ukrainian military had no right to call themselves Ukrainians. Recently, however, after a court case, she was reinstated, and in the autumn Farion would have gone back to teaching Ukrainian language and literature and, probably, her political persuasions to students.

For some time before her death, most commentators had stopped taking Farion's statements seriously. They seemed designed to scandalise but did not affect political or social developments within the country. However, among radical defenders of the Ukrainian language, Farion was seen as a leader. Perhaps that is why the news of her murder made some Ukrainian activists look for traces of Russian involvement in the crime. Evidence of this may be found eventually, but, for now, suspicion has been fixed on an eighteen-year-old man from the city of Dnipro, in south-eastern Ukraine, who sat near her house for two weeks before the murder, dressed so brightly that it was impossible not to notice him. Plenty of witnesses remembered seeing him. He was even photographed. He made no attempt to conceal his presence and sometimes even communicated with Farion's neighbours in good Ukrainian.

After the murder, it took the police only two days to find him, and the investigators were rewarded with trophy pistols for their quick work – a fact that outraged veterans of the Russian–Ukrainian war, who said that the defenders of Mariupol and other heroes had not been rewarded so handsomely.

Copious details about the eighteen-year-old detainee, Vyacheslav Zinchenko, are already known. He is interested in football and, according to investigators, is a patriot who killed Farion because he believed her activities were dividing Ukrainian society. The investigators also insist that Zinchenko was planning another murder – that of the "pro-Russian Deputy" Max Buzhansky – for the same reason. Buzhansky represents political views diametrically opposed to Farion's, although he considers himself a patriot of Ukraine and an opponent of the Kremlin and Putin.

There remain a great many questions around this story. The murder weapon has not been discovered. No traces of gunpowder were found on Zinchenko's hands or clothes. And why would he sit around for weeks making himself so conspicuous if his plan was to kill someone? Poirot would have had a field day, but ordinary Ukrainians, tired of waiting for investigators to find the real culprit have turned their attention to Tuareg music. The ability to switch attention quickly from one topic to another could be a sign of a traumatised, neurasthenic psyche. It is also notable that Ukrainian social media shows a low level of interest in the Paris Olympic Games. I wonder what psychological deviation this may indicate.

Iryna Farion's supporters are not so easily distracted. They have demanded that Lviv University be renamed after her. Since 1940 the university has borne the name of the Ukrainian classic writer Ivan Franko. He was a powerful political and public figure when Lviv was part of the Austro-Hungarian Empire. Farion supporters have also requested that she be awarded the title of "Hero of Ukraine" and that a city street be named after her. Lviv's Mayor has promised that an Iryna Farion Street will appear in western Ukraine's unofficial capital.

In the meantime, Ukrainians from all walks of life are discovering Tuareg music with great interest. I spent an hour or so listening to it myself and rather enjoyed it. Especially the group Tinariwen. I have added it to my playlist. If you haven't listened to it yet, I can recommend it. In addition to catchy melodies, the music has an almost magical calming effect and can distract you from unnerving news.

13.08.2024

Return to Kursk

On August 6, when all of Ukraine was nervously following the slow but steady advance of Russian troops in Donbas, out of the blue came the news of the Ukrainian army's incursion into Russia's Kursk Oblast.

At first, Russian media talked about a "border provocation in which up to 1,000 Ukrainian troops with a small number of armoured vehicles are participating", but on August 8, the same Russian media reported that battles between Russian and Ukrainian units were taking place 22 kilometres inside Russia, near the town of Sudzha.

For the first two days of the operation ordinary Ukrainians could not get a clear picture of what was happening. Many citizens were outraged by the move, questioning how the army had been able to launch an incursion into Russia when there were not enough soldiers to defend Kharkiv region and Donbas. There was a reasonable fear that our troops could be encircled; that there could be issues with the supply of ammunition and fuel. Since then, the mood has calmed, and most Ukrainians have resigned themselves to monitoring yet another front – this one on the territory of the Russian Federation.

Kursk occupies a special place in Soviet Second World War history. The city of Kursk gave its name to the largest tank battle ever known. The Battle of Kursk, in 1943, lasted

50 days and involved up to two million soldiers, 4,000 aircraft, 6,000 tanks and countless other vehicles. The battle thwarted the plans of the German Command and was a turning point in the war for the U.S.S.R. Could this be why Kursk region was chosen for a summer offensive? A more practical explanation is that Kursk is the area from which Russia almost every day attacks Ukraine's Sumy and Chernihiv regions with missiles and heavy bombs.

The new "Battle of Kursk" is on a very different scale from that of 1943, but its impact on the military and political situation in Russia has already shown itself to be significant. Russian officials are prohibited from commenting to journalists about it. Putin himself called the invasion a provocation by terrorists, but, at the same time, references to the 1943 battle are already being used by the Russian propaganda machine to raise the spirits of the Kursk residents who are being evacuated and to calm other Russians who are stunned by this unexpected turn of events.

One notable aspect of the incursion is the number of Russian soldiers who have been taken prisoner – more than 1,000 mostly young soldiers who were drafted into the army and deployed along the border with Ukraine. There are some fighters from the infamous Chechen "Akhmat" battalion as well, but it is the sheer number of prisoners that could prove to be a logistical issue for the Ukrainian army. Somehow, they have to be processed and sent back into Ukraine.

As the Ukrainian military is starting to build fortifications on the captured Russian territory, it seems clear that this operation is not a P.R. stunt or some kind of diversionary manoeuvre. Rather, it seems to have longer-term goals. The Ukrainian Command, no doubt, hopes that Russia will transfer troops from the eastern front to defend Kursk region. Ukraine could be planning to hold on to part of Kursk region as a bargaining chip in negotiations on ending the war.

The most surprising thing for me, and probably for many other Ukrainians, is that preparations for such a complex military operation went unnoticed by Russian intelligence and Ukrainians alike. The planning must have been wide-ranging, and yet there were no leaks of information, and this indicates a new level of sophistication in Ukrainian military operations. According to the Deputy of the Russian State Duma, General Andrei Gurulev, Russian intelligence warned the political elite about the invasion 48 hours before it began. The Kremlin, apparently, did not believe it. Putin has, once again, been shaking the chair of his Chief of the General Staff, General Gerasimov, entrusting the job of squeezing the Ukrainian army out of Kursk to the F.S.B., under the control of his one-time bodyguard and the current Secretary of the State Council of Russia, Aleksey Dyumin, who just happens to have been born in Kursk, 51 years ago. This means that the Russian army officers in the operation will not be reporting to their own commanders. There has long been thinly veiled animosity between the army and the F.S.B., and this new arrangement could bring those rifts to the surface.

In Ukraine, we can expect grandiose bombings of our cities as Putin seeks to take revenge. It has proved increasingly difficult for Ukraine to repel mass missile and drone attacks using available air defence systems, but the arrival of F-16 fighter jets – long ago promised by the Airforce Capability Coalition for Ukraine (America, the Netherlands and Denmark) – could help to counter the cruise missiles launched by Russian strategic aviation. Indeed, the availability of the F-16s may have been important in the timing of the Ukrainian incursion into Kursk region.

I would like to believe, of course, that there will be no reprisals. But after each of Ukraine's military successes, Russia has shelled our cities and killed civilians in unrestrained attacks. This is a stable algorithm. Even before the air raid warning sounds, I have a premonition of another shelling. Such heightened intuition negatively affects the nervous system. We all need something to distract us from our terrifying reality.

*

In March of this year, an interesting decision was made by the management of the National Museum of the History of Ukraine in the Second World War. They dismantled a large copper frieze depicting the 1943 Battle of Kursk. This piece of Soviet monumental art – four metres high and fifteen metres long – was the main exhibit in one of the museum's halls and is certainly one of the best examples of propaganda art from the period. I wonder what the museum plans to put in its place. One suggestion is a new work by the well-known Kyiv artist Evgeniya Gapchinska: a portrait of General Budanov, the head of Ukraine's Main Intelligence Directorate in the Ministry of Defence. It is not an ordinary, ceremonial portrait with medals and shoulder straps. Quite the opposite, it shows Budanov with his pet toad Petya, who recently turned seventeen.

In her art, Gapchinska has a very special way of transposing characters into a soft and childlike world. Her paintings are often used in the design of candy boxes and greeting cards. Some of her colleagues may consider her work too commercial, but her technique is masterful, and ordinary Ukrainians are delighted by it.

The portrait of General Budanov begs to be put on a large box of chocolates, but while Budanov himself has expressed satisfaction with the painting, he probably would not want to see it on candy wrappers, which would be following the Soviet tradition of having chocolate bars named after war heroes. For example, there were Chapaev sweets in honour of the Red Army commander who was killed by White Army soldiers in September 1919.

The war has seriously affected Gapchinska's own family. Her husband, Dima, was drafted into the army in the spring of 2022 and since then he has had only a few, short periods of leave. His first visit home shocked Evgeniya. Nothing in her previous life had prepared her to see her husband as a war-hardened soldier. As Evgeniya recalls, Dima brought with him the smell of war, the smell of death. He had simply had nowhere to take a shower before entering the apartment.

At that time, their country house near Bucha was in a dilapidated state, having been looted and disfigured by Russian occupiers. Evgeniya has worked to restore it. Dima was recently injured at the front, but he is convalescing and preparing to return to his unit.

Evgeniya's story, together with the portrait of General

Budanov, would fit nicely into the empty space in the museum, but the Soviet copper frieze will more likely be replaced by an exhibit dedicated to the 2024–5 Battle of Kursk. It could be called "Kursk Two" or "Return to Kursk". Any exhibit is bound to feature General Budanov, since detachments from his department are engaged in the operation and he no doubt had some part in planning it.

Sooner or later, we will learn more of how the operation came about and the rationale behind it. It will be noted in our museums and in future textbooks about Ukraine's modern history.

23.08.2024

Thoughts on the Eve of Independence Day

Lately, the sceptic in me has been fighting with the optimist, and sometimes the sceptic wins.

Yet another delay in the delivery of military aid from our allies has made me wonder whether some of these hold-ups are deliberate. The war is dragging on. For the third time, Ukraine must celebrate its Independence Day under fire from rockets and drones, glued to reports from the front lines.

There is a heavy sense of a total slowdown, from the delivery of military aid to the implementation of plans to restore destroyed homes and businesses. It seems impossible to imagine any dynamic action – anything that could bring a sudden halt to this war or change its course for the better.

Ukrainian forces are advancing in Kursk region, promising to leave when the time comes. The Russian army is advancing in Donbas, but they will not voluntarily abandon captured territories, at least not until there is regime change in Moscow.

For a brief moment, the flare of the Kursk operation brought Ukrainian society to life, but already we are once more frozen in tense observation of the Russian army's advances in the east.

Morale, nonetheless, remains firm. There is no depression or despair. Ukrainians who have chosen to stay in their country are hopeful of a positive outcome to the war. They may be wary of concepts like "victory" and the "complete liberation of occupied territories" and yet, if asked, patriotic self-censorship will stifle any doubts about an eventual win for Ukraine.

Each Ukrainian resists the enemy with whatever they have at their disposal – the military with weapons, civilians with a stubborn faith in victory. A faith that turns Independence Day into an almost religious festival.

I look forward to August 24, believing it will lend me and all Ukrainians further strength and confidence in our future.

27.08.2024

Moths, Cockroaches and a "Nobel Prize"

During a missile attack in Kharkiv the other day, a man carried a large, rolled-up carpet out of his apartment building and hung it on a horizontal bar in the yard. He then proceeded to attack it with a carpet-beater. This simple action attracted the attention of dozens of neighbours who, instead of running to a bomb shelter or hiding in their hallways, chose to record the process on their mobile phones. The video instantly spread across social networks and raised the spirits of people who were sheltering from another ferocious attack. I saw it too and I could not help but smile. In the cleaning of a carpet during an air raid, I recognised something more than an open challenge to the Russian aggressors. There was great irony in this action.

When Putin served in the K.G.B., he earned the nickname "Moth" because he was very inconspicuous and, of course, physically small. For house-proud Soviet people carpets were a status symbol. They hung them on their walls and defended them from moths by any means possible. The most popular practice was carpet beating, but a chemical agent called naphthalene was a trusted ally in the fight. I still remember its rather unpleasant smell being omnipresent in Soviet apartments.

Another enemy that invaded the homes of Soviet people was the cockroach. This pest had to be combated even more vehemently than the moth. Against cockroaches, no weapon was entirely successful, and they remained a blight on Ukrainian homes long after independence. When my wife and I purchased an apartment for our growing family in the mid-1990s, it was filled with them. The place had to be fumigated for three days before renovation work could begin.

The cockroaches lived primarily in the kitchen and the bathroom, but you could find them in bedrooms too. They lodged under the furniture, beneath the parquet, under the wallpaper. Perhaps aptly, "Cockroach" is the nickname of the illegitimate President of Belarus, Alexander Lukashenko. This is how the Belarusian people depict him in their caricatures – the nasty pest of which they cannot rid themselves.

Perhaps it is not surprising that the Russian "Moth" and the Belarusian "Cockroach" have united against pro-European Ukraine. These pests are desperate to drag our country back into the miserable Soviet past, filled with censorship, fake ideology and the daily battle against moths and cockroaches.

On August 26, while a resident of Kharkiv was beating his carpet, Russia targeted Ukraine with 127 missiles and 109 drones, continuing the attack for more than ten hours. This must have been the most wide-ranging assault since the war began. Two missiles were shot down over the usually safe region of Zakarpattia. The Russian army tries to avoid this area so as not to upset Putin's friend, Hungarian Prime Minister Orban. Thanks to Ukrainian air defence, there were no casualties in Zakarpattia, and no drones or missiles entered Hungarian airspace. However, one drone flew into Polish airspace and there were casualties in fifteen Ukrainian regions, including Kyiv.

Summer is ending dynamically and in blazing heat. We seem to be heading towards a peak in the recent escalation. Without giving any details, Putin's press secretary Peskov announced that Putin had come up with a way to respond to Ukraine's seizure of part of Kursk region. Reprisal attacks were expected on August 24, Ukraine's Independence Day, but they came two days later and seem to herald the beginning of a wave of attacks that will continue into the autumn, accompanied by all kinds of manoeuvres by Russia and its ally Belarus.

On August 25, we looked tensely towards the Belarusian border where Belarusian troops and equipment as well as detachments of Russian Wagner Group mercenaries had gathered. Some form of provocation was expected and the Ukrainian government demanded that President Lukashenko withdraw all forces from the border, but the attacks came from inside Russia and the territory of annexed Crimea.

On August 24, Ukraine's Independence Day, Russia carried out a pinpoint shelling with high-precision missiles, targeting the Sapphire Hotel in Kramatorsk frequented by foreign and Ukrainian journalists. A Reuters security consultant, British citizen Ryan Evans, was killed and the agency's Ukrainian cameraman was seriously wounded. Five other journalists suffered minor injuries.

We have a catalogue of these precisely aimed strikes, the victims of which are civilians, primarily journalists and prominent public figures. A year ago, a similar missile destroyed a pizzeria in Kramatorsk, where Ukrainian writer Victoria Amelina was fatally wounded. A group of Latin American journalists and writers who were with Amelina miraculously escaped without serious injury. Earlier still, a Russian missile had hit the platform of Kramatorsk train station, where hundreds of city residents were waiting for an evacuation train. About 70 civilians were killed, mostly women and children.

In these targeted attacks, Russia is still trying to assassinate people who are known for their pro-Ukrainian and pro-European positions. A Russian missile recently hit the home of the president of Kharkiv University, Tetyana Kaganovska. She was not in the house. Soon afterwards, a missile hit the home of a well-known Kharkiv businessman and volunteer, Yuriy Sopronov. He and his family were out, but the building was destroyed. Ilya Ponomarev, the former Deputy of the Russian State Duma who fled to Ukraine, was less fortunate. An Iranian drone loaded with 40 kilograms of explosives flew straight into the window of his home near Kyiv. Ponomarev suffered multiple shrapnel injuries but survived.

The regular use of missiles and drones for these pinpoint operations may seem strange, but it is part of a Soviet tradition and proof of the K.G.B.'s hand in the planning of this war. The K.G.B.'s operating principle can be summed up in four words: "No person – no problem!" It would, however, be a mistake to assume that nobody in Russia's political elite thinks of anything except the eradication of Ukrainians who motivate their country to fight for independence and a European future. Russia continues to enjoy a Kafkaesque cultural and social life based on the "fundamental values" of Russian Orthodoxy which gives Russia the praise for all positive developments and shuns interference from foreign influences. At the same time, Russia craves the prestige of some aspects of Western culture, always manipulating them to highlight Russia's glory. For example, even before the war, the Russian State Duma forbade the use of the term "Champagne" for any beverage except Russian sparkling wine. France did not protest and began to sell its beverage as sparkling wine. A less well-known example of this phenomenon involves a "Nobel Prize". In mid-August, a "Nobel Prize" delegation arrived in the capital of Chechnya to award the honour to the Head of the Chechen Republic, Hero of Russia Ramzan Kadyrov. No, it was not a group from the Swedish Academy. It was a delegation from the committee that hands out the Ludvig Nobel Prize which was invented in Russia in 2005 so that Russian V.I.P.s could feel good about themselves.

Ludvig Nobel was the older brother of Alfred. When he was eleven years old Ludvig moved to St Petersburg with his father, who built several factories there and was involved in the oil industry and the development of the railways. His father returned to Sweden, but Ludvig remained with his brother Robert, and became a prominent figure in the world of engineering and business.

In the small mountain village of Sterc-Ketch, Chechnya, the only monument to the Nobel brothers in Russia was unveiled in 2020. The location boasts a "Nobel Trail" – a 3.5-kilometre trail to the oil field discovered by Ludwig Nobel and his business team. Perhaps this is why Ramzan Kadyrov became a laureate of the fake "Nobel Prize". By the way, President Putin received this prize in 2008, but it is not known exactly what he received it for. While Ramzan Kadyrov is happy to call himself a Nobel laureate, his forces continue to participate in military operations within Ukraine and in Kursk region of the Russian Federation.

*

Evacuation trains are once more travelling from Donbas to western Ukraine, particularly from Pokrovsk, a city that is only ten kilometres from the front line – and that distance is getting shorter. The trains are overcrowded, and the refugees evacuate with heavy hearts and very few belongings. Almost everything is left behind, including furniture and carpets. At the same time, carpets are travelling in the opposite direction. In Zakarpattia, volunteers are calling on local residents to bring their old carpets to collection points where they are checked for moths, cleaned and sent east, to Donbas, Kharkiv and Zaporizhzhia regions. It may be hot now, but the cold weather is approaching. The dugouts and fortifications along the front line must be made more comfortable for soldiers. More than 300 carpets were recently dispatched from the town of Mukachevo. They will cover the beaten-earth floors of fortifications and dugouts. This will be the carpets' last heroic role, the final use for this former cult object of Soviet life.

Meanwhile, Ukrainian farmers and smallholders are digging up potatoes, harvesting grain and seeking the best storage opportunities to keep their produce fresh until the spring. Life in Ukraine continues as Russia's full-scale aggression ploughs past its first 900 days.

10.09.2024

Counting on Our Military Engineers

The watermelon season is nearly over. There were none on sale in our local town Brusiliv in Zhytomyr region last Sunday, but a neighbour brought us one of his own. Home-grown watermelons have become a common feature in local gardens. They are sweet enough, but even with the blazing heat we have had this year they only grow to the size of a bowling ball.

The last week of August and the first week of September dealt heavy blows to our summer optimism. First, we were numbed by the deaths of more than 60 mobilised soldiers on the territory of the military communications school in Poltava, targeted by ballistic missiles. Another 300 soldiers were wounded. Then there was the shelling of apartment blocks in Lviv which killed almost the entire family of one of the descendants of a classic of Ukrainian literature, Ivan Franko. Only the father survived.

These tragedies seemed to trigger some long-promised – but not particularly eagerly awaited – personnel changes in government. The news from Poltava and Lviv was pushed aside by coverage of the shake-up. Several ministers and senior officials resigned, including Foreign Minister Dmytro Kuleba. Dismissals and new appointments in the Office of the President were also announced. Ukrainians looked on bemused. The names involved in the reshuffle are unfamiliar to most people. The outgoing officials were not known for any memorable public policies or noted for outstanding service, but the new names mean even less. We feel obliged to pay some attention to developments in the corridors of power, but news from the front remains more important.

As Parliament voted on the changes in the Cabinet, the news broke that the National Bank was planning to change the name of Ukraine's smallest denomination. The familiar kopeck will be replaced by the shag, meaning "step". The change was presented as another move towards Europe and away from the Russian/Soviet tradition of roubles and kopecks.

Shags were in circulation briefly in 1918 after Ukraine declared its independence. Like today, there was a war going on. Ukraine was trying to protect its independence while Russia was dragging the country into a new Russian Empire – the Soviet Union. Shag coins were never minted. They were printed on cheap paper cut into small squares and they looked more like postage stamps than money. No-one took them seriously then, and today news of their reintroduction has been met with incomprehension. While branches of Ukrainian banks are moving their equipment out of settlements situated anywhere near the front line, can reforms of this type be a priority?

Introducing the coin at this juncture seems inappropriate also from a socio-psychological point of view and yet social media is full of discussions on the topic. Some people are already dreaming of adding the new shag to their numismatic collections. Others are wondering whose image will be on the coins. There is no official information available, only a vague statement from the National Bank buttressed by rumours. For ordinary Ukrainians, only one thing is clear: food prices and electricity tariffs are rising and neither kopecks nor shags will help.

One euro cent is worth 45 kopecks. A box of matches costs 70 kopecks. So, the new coin could only be of interest to collectors. It is not for nothing that the one-, two-, five- and 25-kopeck coins were withdrawn before 2022, leaving only the ten- and 50-kopeck coins in circulation. At that same time coins worth one, two, five and ten hryvnias were introduced.

Discussions about kopecks on T.V. and radio have been overshadowed by news from the United States: the five and a half billion dollars allocated for aid to Ukraine have not been transferred. Bloggers have reacted with noisy pessimism and in an attempt to counter their comments, journalists from official T.V. channels are insisting that the money has not yet been lost and that, in any case, it is not such a large sum. What seems certain is that the money must be spent on military aid for Ukraine by the end of September or it will be returned to the U.S. Treasury.

War is thousands of times more expensive than peace – a seemingly bottomless pit. One day of war costs Ukraine approximately one hundred million dollars. So, five and a half billion dollars would allow the country to defend itself for 55 days. I have never liked mathematics, but this war forces me to do arithmetic all the time. I am forever counting the number of destroyed Russian tanks and planes, the number of Iranian drones shot down over Kyiv every night, the number of F-16s expected in Ukraine by the end of 2024.

The other day, I got help solving a slightly more complex problem. At 3 a.m., an explosion lit up the sky outside our apartment in Kyiv. We heard the sound of the explosion five seconds later. I wanted to know how far away from our house the Russian drone had exploded. I posed this question on my Twitter page and soon received an answer from one of my readers – the explosion occurred 1.7 kilometres from us. The speed of sound is 343 metres per second. Remember this; you may need it.

The mathematics of war is not only about counting the enemy's losses in equipment and personnel. It means calculating the enemy's remaining and renewable resources. This year already, 190,000 men in the Russian Federation have signed contracts to participate in the aggression against Ukraine. Some of these contract soldiers are convicted criminals who have been allowed to fight instead of sitting in prison. Some of the others are homeless people. Representatives of the Russian armed forces recently began visiting homeless shelters in Siberia and elsewhere, encouraging residents to sign a contract that would offer them a high salary and a new home: the Russian army. The number of Russian homeless who have chosen to change their status in this way is not known.

Above all else, the Russian army needs infantry soldiers – cannon fodder for storming the Ukrainian fortifications along the front line. I do not suppose that the homeless folk who are being recruited are told about that. I imagine they see themselves serving away from the front or, at worst, as drone operators. As well as increasing drone production, Russia is developing new types of drones. Ukraine has also raised its output of this essential tool in modern warfare and broadened the range of drones it produces. Last week,

Ukrainian operators were able to use a locally produced drone to shoot down a Russian reconnaissance drone at a record altitude of 3.5 kilometres.

Russia attacks us around the clock with Iranian Shahed drones. These weapons can stay in the air for ten hours or more, often changing direction. Drone terror keeps Ukrainians on the edge of their seats all day and in their corridors most nights. Nobody gets proper sleep, but lately, something strange has been happening. Some of the enemy's drones have flown out of Ukrainian airspace and into Belarus, causing panic among Belarusian air defence squads. The first time it happened, the Belarusian military only monitored the movement of the Russian drone. It flew into Belarus but then turned around and flew back into Ukraine. When Russian drones started falling on Belarus, however, "President" Lukashenko decreed that the country's air defences must shoot down any foreign drones in Belarusian airspace regardless of their country of origin. So, Belarusian anti-aircraft guns are shooting down Iranian drones that Russia intended for Ukraine. According to Russian military bloggers, the Kremlin is not happy about Lukashenko's decree. This may result in Belarus facing obstacles in the purchase of Russian gas and oil.

Russian bloggers say that Putin is insisting that Belarus refrain from shooting down the "Shaheds". Putin also wants Lukashenko to return Belarusian troops to the Ukrainian border and to keep alive the threat of attacks from there. Lukashenko, however, seems in no hurry to carry out Putin's wishes.

The wayward drones that have caused a new rift between

Minsk and Moscow may be the result of work by Ukrainian electronic warfare specialists who have learned to reprogramme Iranian drones as they fly over Ukraine, redirecting them into Belarus. This does not entirely explain the case of the Iranian drone carrying 40 kilograms of explosives that crashed in Latvia at the end of last week. It was flying from Russia. Fortunately, it did not explode. Latvia stated that Russia had not planned an attack against Latvia and that it was an unfortunate military accident. The Lithuanian government took the incident more seriously and is drawing up plans for the evacuation of settlements close to the border with Belarus.

Meanwhile, in Ukraine, some positive news has been generated. Ukrainians are now able to get married online through the "Diya" (Action) application which is controlled by government agencies and allows Ukrainian citizens to obtain a range of electronic documents. Getting married online takes only 30 minutes and the newlyweds immediately receive state marriage certificates in electronic format, while the paper version will be sent to them by post.

The "Diya" application does not yet generate divorce papers. Couples will have to sever their relationships in the traditional way: through the courts or the Department of Marriages, Births and Deaths.

25.09.2024

Public Desertion and Going Home to Die

On September 21, a "bomb" exploded in Ukraine. This time it did not come from Russia. Hundreds of Russian bombs are dropped on Ukrainian cities and towns every day. They do not always make it into the news any more. They are our normality.

The "bomb" that exploded on September 21 was a home-made "information bomb". But the "blast" has shaken our society, which is already exhausted, radicalised and very tired of war.

The "explosion" occurred when the well-known public activist, blogger and founder of the literary festival "Vydelka Fest", Sergiy Gnezdilov, announced that after five years of service in the Ukrainian armed forces, including many months on the front line, he was "leaving the location of his military unit without permission and ending his military service". That is to say, he was publicly deserting from the Ukrainian army.

He chose this course of action to set off an open debate about the regulation of demobilisation instructions which do not exist on paper or in practice.

Gnezdilov's startling move has divided active elements within Ukrainian society. There are those who support him and those who denounce him as a provocateur and a traitor. But it must be said that even the negative reactions have been tempered. It is understood that the topic of mobilisation and demobilisation is very painful for every serviceman in the Ukrainian army.

In 2019, Gnezdilov chose to take academic leave from Lviv University, where he was studying to be a journalist, to volunteer for the armed forces and contribute to the defence of Ukraine's sovereignty. He served in the hottest spots of the war: in Pesky near Donetsk and in Bakhmut. But after five years of service and war, he has come to the end of his tether. At a discussion during the Festival of Ideas in Kyiv, he announced his decision to unilaterally end his military service. "The authorities have decided to withdraw from this issue, precious time has been lost. It is not the nation that goes to the front, but the losers, those who were caught by military enlistment officers. Right now, muscly guys in gyms are boasting to each other about how much [money] they paid and to whom, to avoid what they call someone else's war. We need decisive action and equality of citizens not only in terms of their rights, but their responsibilities as well. We are losing territory and precious time due to the criminal inaction of the authorities."

His words did not provoke condemnation in Ukrainian society because they ring true and the picture Gnezdilov paints resembles our reality.

In the minds of patriotic Ukrainians, Kyiv and Lviv's packed cafés and bars are no longer associated with a brave civilian population determined to show they will not be beaten by air raids and power outages. Today, the sight of nightclub-goers, men having their beards trimmed in barber shops, and others working up a sweat in fitness centres gives rise to indignation and doubt about the fairness of the mobilisation strategy.

According to the law, every man between the ages of eighteen and 60 must carry his military I.D. with him, but in central areas of Kyiv, enlistment officers do not stop and check passers-by. That does happen, however, in other towns and villages, and on the highways between them. The humiliating term "busification" is heard increasingly often. It refers to the process of forcibly detaining men on the street, placing them in a "bus" and delivering them to a mobilisation centre from where there is only one road – to an army training ground. The term is already used by Members of Parliament, although it sounds offensive both to representatives of the army and to the victims of this manhunt procedure.

Enlistment officers who are on the front line of mobilisation are perceived by many Ukrainians as enemies – as inherently corrupt back-office personnel. Unlike combat soldiers, enlistment officials are treated without respect and sometimes with outright hostility. In recent months, during street document checks and "busification" procedures, hundreds of violent incidents have been reported. Officers have been attacked, some have had their cars burned or have received threats. As a result, they have been given the right to use firearms and to shoot to kill if they believe their lives are in danger.

After several high-profile corruption scandals, the government has tried to improve the image of enlistment officers. War veterans who could no longer fight because of injury have been moved into the enlistment services. However, they are still using the old methods. "Busification" has not been replaced by anything less humiliating and society's attitude towards enlistment officers has not changed.

A well-known lawyer and serviceman, Masi Nayem, joined the discussion about Gnezdilov's public desertion, saying: "Firstly, it is immoral in relation to those who have died or were wounded. They gave their lives and health to prevent the front lines from being surrendered to the enemy. It is also unfair to your brothers-in-arms who remain on the front line, in service! It is a great pity that society has absolved itself of responsibility for the war, believing that donations and posts on Facebook are enough!"

Nayem admitted, however, that the lack of demobilisation rules and procedures is causing increasingly heated debate and frustration. Other commentators have accused Gnezdilov of contributing to the growth in the number of deserters. Some estimates put the figure at 80,000, but this may be an exaggeration. During 2023, only 1,577 servicemen were convicted of desertion in Ukraine.

This discussion is being monitored by hundreds of thousands of servicemen at the front and millions of civilians. Gnezdilov knows that he broke the laws and that for unauthorised abandonment of his unit he could get from five to twelve years in prison. It seems that he is ready for this. On September 23, the Prosecutor General's Office announced the opening of a criminal case based on Gnezdilov's statement about his decision unilaterally to end his military service. So far, however, he has not been arrested. Instead, there have been attempts to talk him round. It is clear that the authorities are waiting for the noise around Gnezdilov's announcement to quieten. Detaining him would cause more excitement and neither the Ministry of Defence nor the Office of the President want this case to gain a higher profile in the public consciousness.

Meanwhile, the funeral of a 39-year-old veteran of the Russian–Ukrainian war, Oleg Latyshev, took place quietly in the ancient town of Ostrog, but it was the very quietness of the ceremony that caused a scandal. To the outrage of all who knew him and who had fought with him at the front, Latyshev's funeral took place without military honours, without the presence of soldiers, and without shots fired over the coffin.

Latyshev took part in military operations in Donbas in 2014–15, and at the beginning of the full-scale war he was called up again. He fought in Bucha, in Sumy region and in Bakhmut, where he was seriously wounded. After eight months in various hospitals, he returned home to Ostrog where he died as a result of the injuries he had endured at the front, just like his brother Taras, who died from wounds a year ago.

The problem is that on his death Latyshev's official status was that of a soldier who had left his unit without permission – that is, a deserter. He was given this status because having left hospital he went straight home instead of returning to his military unit to deal with the paperwork associated with demobilisation due to injury.

The figure of 80,000 deserters could include servicemen who, having spent months in hospitals trying to hold on to life, did not have the strength to return to their military units to apply for demobilisation on health grounds and simply went home to die.

In April of this year, Parliament adopted a law on mobilisation which was to include an article making demobilisation possible after 36 months of military service. However, this article was removed from the draft law at the request of Defence Minister Umerov and the Commander-in-Chief of the Ukrainian Armed Forces, General Syrsky. This caused indignation among soldiers, and they were promised a separate law on demobilisation. To date, no such law has appeared.

10.10.2024

War and the Psyche

A number of Russian politicians recently decided to open a new front – one targeting their own citizens, specifically those who provide "magic services", for example, sorcerers, astrologers, tarot readers and other fortune tellers and healers. State Duma Deputy Alexander Spiridonov is about to put the finishing touches to a bill that, if adopted, would ban not only the advertising of "magic services" but even the mention of them and those who provide such services in the media. Anyone continuing to work in this field will face criminal charges and could be sentenced to a couple of years in prison.

This law would impact not only service providers but also a segment of higher education. Russian astrologers are taught and trained by several private universities, including the Moscow Academy of Astrology, which opened in 1990, just before the break-up of the Soviet Union. It and similar establishments would have to close or diversify.

A course of study to become an astrologer in Russia usually lasts four years. Spiridonov, who actively supports the war against Ukraine and regularly visits the occupied territories, wants to leave all the professionals in the sector without work. Perhaps he hopes that, in desperation, the unemployed prophets and seers will sign contracts with the Russian army and go to fight Ukraine.

*

Today is World Mental Health Day and a good opportunity to focus on the severe psychological burden that Ukrainians now bear and the way we try to deal with it. Since the end of last year, the Ukrainian Parliament has been awaiting discussion of a bill to regulate "esoteric services", which include a range of activities, from yoga classes to tarot reading. The bill aims to regulate the accreditation of educational courses for these professions and the selection and preparation of trainers who will have to complete periods of teaching practice.

A new category will have to be created in Ukraine's professional classification documentation so that service providers can register as private entrepreneurs and pay tax. The author of the bill is Serhiy Grivko, a deputy from the Servant of the People party. He believes that bringing these professions into the regulated economy will raise about 100 million hryvnias (approximately £1.85 million) in tax – enough to buy an Abrams tank or four missiles for H.I.M.A.R.S. systems.

A bill like this may seem untimely during a war, but esoteric services have suddenly become relevant due to a public outcry over the "Mother of God". The scandal concerns a woman who goes by that name and who purports to have special powers that, among other things, enable her to keep wounded soldiers alive. Activists who help the families of dead, injured and missing soldiers have sought legal advice on how to prevent Anna Fesun (her real name) from exploiting soldiers' relatives and friends who believe in her powers and give her money. No legal action, however, can be taken against this woman without a statement from her victims and the people who trust Fesun to find or heal their relatives do not see themselves as such. Indeed, they actively defend the "Mother of God".

Against this background, the regulation of "esoteric services" becomes an urgent matter and part of the drive to protect the nation's mental health. In February of this year, the Ministry of Health adopted a new, expanded list of circumstances in which Ukrainians can access free psychological and psychiatric services. The list includes afflictions caused by military action, forced relocation and the death or injury of a loved one. In my experience, people who find themselves in difficulty rarely turn to psychologists or psychiatrists. They prefer to believe in miracles. I wonder whether the regulation of esoteric services will help to strengthen this trend or weaken it.

Over the last two and half years, Ukrainian citizens have had to face enormous stress and tragedy every day. They have become accustomed to sharing bad news on their social media pages – fertile ground for the seeds of depression. The root cause of our sadness is Russia's aggression. Russia knows how to feed depression and how to use it as a weapon. Russian troops regularly gun down Ukrainian soldiers who have surrendered, filming the murders and posting the videos on Telegram and Facebook. Ukrainians, shocked by what they see, repost the videos on social media, and the horror spreads yet further.

The Russian army's capture of the city of Vuhledar in Donbas has been a massive blow to Ukrainians. Equally shocking was the highly publicised suicide of the battalion commander of the 123rd Territorial Defence Brigade, Lieutenant Colonel Igor Hryb, who defended Vuhledar. The precise circumstances of his death remain unclear. The Ministry of Defence has launched an investigation. Few, though, believe that it will be sufficiently thorough or that the findings will be made public. The truth may come out only after the war, if then.

Mental stress experienced by Ukrainian soldiers on the front line is much more destructive to the psyche than the problems faced by civilians. According to military staffing rules, each battalion – between 400 and 800 soldiers – should have one officer-psychologist. This person should monitor the relationships between soldiers, help avoid conflicts and provide psychological assistance, especially after military action. Even if an officer-psychologist is able to monitor an entire battalion, these officers also take part in military action and can themselves suffer from combat stress and post-traumatic stress disorder. This makes it very difficult to say that there is effective psychological support for soldiers in combat zones.

For civilians, the best cure for depression is good news from the front. The capture of part of Russia's Kursk region provided a dose of positivity, but that pill is no longer efficacious. Hopes are being pinned on President Zelensky's recently announced "victory plan" which needs to be a realistic road map to peace, rather than a temporary cure for depression in Ukrainian society. Without giving any details, President Zelensky has mentioned his plan in addresses to the nation and we know that the Ukrainian leadership is waiting for a reaction to it from the U.S. presidential administration. President Zelensky promises to reveal selected details of the plan to Ukrainian citizens if it gets the thumbs up from the White House, but part of the plan will necessarily remain classified.

The hype around this plan together with its mysterious content makes it seem more like a "cure for depression" than a real action plan. But who knows? Perhaps the Ukrainian leadership has prepared two victory plans: a real plan of military and political action and a second plan designed to calm citizens who are tired of negative news. We can hope that all will be revealed soon enough, removing the need to turn to the "Mother of God" or other astrologers and magicians to discover what is going on.

By the way, the ban on "magic services" proposed by Russian State Duma Deputy Alexander Spiridonov is most unlikely to pass into law. President Putin has been communicating with shamans for twenty years, consulting with them on many issues, including military action in Ukraine. Following the example of their President, Russia's most prominent businesspeople and oligarchs also make use of seers, astrologers and shamans, even hiring them to work in the recruitment sections of their H.R. departments.

23.10.2024

Nuclear Dreams and Reality

Last Monday, visitors to the central park in Vinnytsia, in south-western Ukraine, may have been surprised to see a large number of people with long metal canes in the area of the park which commemorates well-known figures from Vinnytsia region. The group spent a long time examining the busts and statues, actively discussing their discoveries. Then they moved on to a monument, placed slightly apart, that was recently brought to Vinnytsia from Pokrovsk – a city in Donetsk region which is gradually being destroyed by Russian bombs and missiles. The monument depicts the figure of Mykola Leontovych, the Ukrainian composer of the well-known Christmas song "Carol of the Bells". The excursion to Vinnytsia's central park was organised by local ophthalmologist Nelya Krivetska together with the local Society for the Blind and Visually Impaired.

Like all Ukrainians, people with impaired sight have faced new and serious challenges since the beginning of the war. Their needs have never been properly met by state infrastructure and, while they do receive support from caring fellow citizens and N.G.O.s, this part of our society remains largely "invisible" to the sighted majority. This has prompted activists to launch a project entitled "Be Visible", designed to increase awareness that there are Ukrainians who "see" the world through touch and sound. Through touch and sound, they perceive the war and deal with all the challenges it inflicts.

Some Ukrainians with impaired sight became refugees in Great Britain and Germany, the U.S. and Canada. The host communities have become a powerful support force for these refugees, as well as for people with impaired sight who remain in Ukraine and for Ukraine as a whole. In their social media chats you can follow members of these communities engaged in all the latest debates. The key topic at the moment is nuclear physics and its laws, particularly the possibility of creating an atomic bomb in makeshift conditions and whether nuclear waste from power plants can be used for this purpose. In short, it seems that the nuclear ambitions which Putin quite improbably accused Ukraine of harbouring at the beginning of the war have become a reality.

Everyone is discussing the 1994 Budapest Memorandum under which Ukraine transferred its nuclear arsenal to Russia in exchange for assurances of the inviolability of the country's borders and the protection of its sovereignty. The guarantors of Ukraine's security under that memorandum were the United States, Russia and Great Britain.

Since then, Ukraine has been considered a non-nuclear state. Recently, however, we were reminded that Ukraine transferred its last 50 kilograms of highly enriched uranium to Russia only in 2010, during the presidency of the pro-Russian Viktor Yanukovych. That enriched uranium – enough to make two nuclear bombs – was flown to Moscow in five planes, distributed between 21 containers. President Obama, who had demanded the transfer, praised Yanukovych for this operation. The U.S. President had feared that Ukraine might, secretly, pass the uranium to Iran or North Korea.

Professional nuclear physicists have already explained to Ukrainians willing to listen why it is impossible to create a nuclear weapon in Ukraine today. Apart from the technical obstacles, there would be huge political consequences. Yan Valetov, the well-known engineer, blogger, writer and activist from Dnipro, shocked his followers by stating that any attempt to create even the smallest atomic bomb would immediately lead to sanctions from the West, the cessation of military and other aid to Ukraine and perhaps, even, a missile strike from our current partners. In making this claim, I assume Valetov was trying to return our nuclear dreamers to their senses.

The topic of nuclear weapons was first raised not by bloggers or activists, but by President Zelensky himself after his "Victory Plan" was criticised by some European allies. At a press conference in Brussels on October 17, President Zelensky mentioned what he had said in a conversation with U.S. presidential candidate Donald Trump: "Either Ukraine will have nuclear weapons, or Ukraine must become a member of N.A.T.O." These words flew around the world and returned to Ukraine at a greatly increased volume, thanks to commentators, journalists and foreign politicians.

Now that we know about the non-secret part of Zelensky's "Victory Plan", we can safely say that it was composed more for the Western political establishment and N.A.T.O. leadership than for Ukrainians. The first point in the plan is immediate accession to N.A.T.O. Ukraine has not yet even been offered a place on the bottom rung of the accession-preparation ladder, let alone accession itself. If the first point in a plan is unattainable then the other points must lose all meaning. The Hungarian and Slovak Prime Ministers openly criticised the plan while the leaders of some of our closest partner countries gently pointed out the poor chances of its being implemented. After this, Zelensky's October 17 statement in Brussels acquired a different, more emotional tone, while Putin immediately declared that Russia would, under no circumstances, permit Ukraine to become a nuclear power.

Zelensky's statement gave a slight boost to his popularity at home, but the loud and optimistic discussions on social networks about the creation of nuclear weapons has darkened the mood of people who know something about nuclear physics.

At a time when public opinion is so fragile, it would seem desirable to set out more realistic plans or at least instructions regarding achievable steps in a positive direction. The Commander-in-Chief of the Armed Forces of Ukraine, General Syrsky, tried his hand at this approach by making a statement about the reform of training for novice fighters. He suggested that training should be extended to at least six weeks. This move could play a positive role, but only if we see a change in the conscription system. "Forced mobilisation" tends to bring negative results, as was confirmed recently in comments by one battalion commander: "Of twenty-five conscripts mobilised off the street by force, only one actually fights. The rest either desert or die in the first few days of their participation in battle," he said.

Russia responded to Ukrainian dreams of nuclear weapons with the news that 12,000 North Korean soldiers were travelling to fight against the Ukrainian army – among them 1,500 from North Korea's elite forces. Russian social networks exploded with admiration for their ally and expressions of faith in the North Korean troops' ability to defeat Ukraine and succeed where the Russian army had failed.

Within a couple of days of the announcement, the number of North Korean soldiers being discussed had shrunk to 3,000 but, since neither North Korea nor Russia will reveal the true extent of the imported force, it could be many more. North Korean troops are already assembling in Kursk region, creating a unique situation in which two nuclear powers are allied against one non-nuclear state. At the same time, we have something that looks like a Ukrainian–North Korean war on Russian territory. No author of dystopian fiction could have come up with such a scenario.

The arrival of North Korean troops in Russia prompted, unfortunately, a wave of xenophobic and cliché-based jokes among Ukrainians which were insulting to Ukrainian Koreans, one of whom – Vitaly Kim – has been the popular and successful governor of the Mykolaiv frontline region for the last four years. However, it has been interesting to see how quickly criticism of the jokes and inaccurate labelling led to self-correction and a desire to stress "North" when talking about bad Koreans.

A day after the news broke about Pyongyang's support to Russia, someone set fire to the Korean restaurant Pan-Syo in Kyiv. It may have been a naive gesture against all things Korean, but the owner is Ilya Bogdanov, a Russian volunteer in the Ukrainian army and a former officer of the Russian secret services who moved to Ukraine in 2014, at the very beginning of this conflict. Ordinary Ukrainians are fundraising to help Bogdanov rebuild his restaurant.

South Korea's leadership cares about what the North Korean army is doing and is carefully watching developments. After all, the war between North and South Korea is not formally over. It has been on pause for many years. Ukraine is anticipating a significant increase in assistance from South Korea, including more military aid.

In the meantime, President Zelensky has announced that he will soon present a new plan – not "Victory Plan mark two" but a strategy that will be based on Ukraine's own resources. This gives some hope that it will be more realistic.

Christmas will be here in two months. Some of you will hear Leontovych's "Carol of the Bells" in church or on the radio. Certainly, it will be sung all over Ukraine during the festive season. The question is whether that joyful sound will drown out the clammer about the country's nuclear dreams.

07.11.2024

Adding Fuel to the Fire

The result of the U.S. presidential election is a major concern for many Ukrainians, but the challenge of keeping warm during the winter looms even larger. Before the war, gas prices rose steeply, and many village residents switched to wood-burning heating systems. Even with the cost of the conversion, people were confident that burning wood would be cheaper than gas, but Parliament has recently voted in favour of a bill that would make life extremely difficult for most people with wood-burning heating systems.

According to the proposed law, if one cubic metre or more of firewood is found in a private yard or shed without proof that it was felled and purchased legally, the property owner will face a large fine. If the wood is oak or pine, the owner could be imprisoned for between five and seven years. News of the bill, which only required President Zelensky's signature to become law, sent shock waves through rural communities, but as Ukrainians woke up to the news of Donald Trump's victory in the U.S. election, Zelensky provided relief for some by announcing that he would not sign the bill on illegal firewood into law.

The cries in defence of the rural population were immediately replaced by shouts of indignation over large-scale, illegal felling of trees and the general lack of forestry management in the country. During the 33 years since independence, chaos and corruption have reigned in this sector of Ukraine's economy. Timber has been cut down on an industrial scale, illegally exported, or sold on the domestic "grey" or "black" markets. From time to time, this problem was discussed in the press, but nothing changed. Against this background, Ukrainians in rural communities feel that they have as much right to the wood growing around them as anyone else.

Christmas tree markets will soon appear all over the country. Some will sell legally felled trees from managed plantations, others will offer trees cut down illegally. For some years, N.G.O.s have organised campaigns to raise awareness of deforestation and convince Ukrainians to buy only barcoded trees produced by forestry enterprises that pay taxes. Thanks to these campaigns, city residents are more likely to buy legal Christmas trees. The situation with firewood, however, has always been more complicated. Buying it legally is generally associated with impenetrable bureaucracy.

"I recently tried to buy firewood for my dacha through official channels," says Viktor Kozhevnikov, a well-known actor and the Director of the Joyfest theatre festival. "I got to the forestry department and waited for the boss to arrive. He turned up three hours later, made a photocopy of my passport and told me to come back the following day. When I returned, he said that the lumberjacks and timber handlers had not shown up for work. They were probably hiding from the military enlistment squads. Anyway, there was no-one to chop firewood. He pointed to an old pear tree in the courtyard and suggested that I cut it down myself and take the wood home."

Stories like this have resulted in the development of the

unofficial firewood market. Along the main approach roads to every Ukrainian town, trucks can be seen with billboards advertising "firewood for sale". House owners simply agree on a price with a driver who then brings the firewood straight to the buyer's home.

It must be said that, in some regions, the market for legally felled firewood is better organised. Larisa Pokalchuk, co-founder of the documentary film studio Babylon-13, bought firewood from the Boryspil forestry office and discovered that legal firewood was two and a half times cheaper than its illegal equivalent.

*

As winter approaches, the cost of heating in both urban and rural areas is one of the factors driving internally displaced persons (I.D.P.s) from the east and south of the country to give up trying to make a life for themselves in the more secure areas of Ukraine and to return home. In recent months, more than 120,000 of them have gone back to the occupied territories. Some have even returned to areas that are still combat zones.

The state has not been able to provide all I.D.P.s with housing. Financial assistance, which was never very generous, has been reduced. It is not always easy for I.D.P.s to find work in an unfamiliar environment. On top of this, the national programme of assistance for internally displaced persons does not include compensation for housing that has been destroyed, damaged or abandoned because of the conflict, while in occupied territories the Russian authorities have increased compensation payments for destroyed or damaged housing. To qualify for this compensation, property owners must first accept Russian citizenship. They then endure a long, bureaucratic process at the end of which, for a destroyed house of 100 square metres, they may receive up to 4,005,000 roubles (about £37,000 as of March 2025).

Since November last year, 320,000 I.D.P.s have tried to return to the occupied territories through Moscow; 200,000 of them were refused entry to Russia and had no choice but to return to Ukraine or become refugees abroad. There are officially more than four million internally displaced persons in Ukraine today. That means four million people who, to a greater or lesser extent, rely on inadequate state programmes of assistance. The number of I.D.P.s may continue to rise as the Russian army lays waste to more areas of eastern and south-eastern Ukraine.

As Ukrainians greet the first snow, we know that winter has already begun, and it promises to be cold and uncomfortable. President Zelensky's refusal to sign the firewood bill is good news for many rural dwellers, but the price of firewood will increase, and the size of Ukraine's forests will shrink.

08.11.2024

After the Shocked Silence

I had the impression that Trump's victory in the U.S. presidential election silenced all of Ukraine. The guns, the tanks and other weapons along the 600 miles of the front line, however, did not fall silent for a minute. Nor was there a pause in the attacks on our cities from Russian missiles and drones, but the news from Washington left the country stunned, enveloped in gut-wrenching disappointment.

This reaction was ensured by forecasts made throughout the campaign by a broad swathe of journalists and political scientists, saying that if Trump won he would halt or greatly reduce military aid to Ukraine and, thereby, force President Zelensky to sit down at the negotiating table with Putin. It is easy to predict the outcome of any such negotiations. Russia demands that the Ukrainian leadership "recognise reality" and give up to Russia not only the areas it has occupied in Ukraine but the entire territories of Zaporizhzhia and Kherson regions, although 50 per cent. of both of those territories are still under Ukrainian control.

The initial shock and despair have faded slightly. Zelensky calmed Ukrainians in his video address to the nation, assuring them that he and Donald Trump have established normal relations and that during a personal meeting in September, the President-Elect had heard everything that the Ukrainian President wanted to tell him.

I choose to believe that Trump's ambition to make America great again is in direct conflict with allowing Putin to make Russia great again. Putin is determined to show that he, and not the American President, can dictate conditions in Central and Eastern Europe and he is working to force N.A.T.O. to accept his dominant position in the region. Putin equates U.S. power with that of N.A.T.O. Trump could undermine Putin's rationale by pulling away from N.A.T.O., but in doing so – in taking an isolationist stance – Trump would be devaluing the U.S. in the eyes of the world and certainly in the eyes of Putin, who will not shirk from demonstrating his superiority over the U.S. President, most likely with a thin smile and wordy statements about how gratifying it is to see that Washington has finally acknowledged its inability to dominate the world.

To allay their fears, Ukrainians would like Trump to address them directly and promise not to abandon their country to Russian domination. This, of course, will not happen, but neither will Zelensky be pushed into unfavourable negotiations with Putin. There will most likely be a reduction in military and other aid coming from Washington. Instead of on Ukraine, Donald Trump will focus his attention on the domestic economy and the situation around Israel. He will hand over the "Ukrainian problem" to the European Union. Thus, Trump's victory in the election will force the E.U. to focus more on its military doctrine and establish a common defence policy. European military aid to Ukraine will not cease, but, as before, it will be delivered with long delays, making it difficult to plan a defence strategy, let alone a broad counteroffensive.

Ultimately, without American aid, Ukraine may find itself in a hopeless situation, and then the only way out of the war will be unfavourable negotiations with Russia. This in turn will lead to even more migration from Ukraine, especially of young people. Ukrainians are not talking about this yet, just as they have not got around to discussing how it was that, among the U.S. Ukrainian diaspora, most of the older generation, like post-Soviet U.S. citizens, voted for Donald Trump in the election. Those voters want a "firm hand" in politics and the economy. In this respect, they somewhat resemble the citizens of the Russian Federation.

18.11.2024

Putin and the Full Moon

"I knew something bad would happen," my sister-in-law, Larisa, told me when I called to check that they were alright.

"How did you know?" I said. For me, Saturday night's missile attack – the first on this scale since the summer – came as a surprise.

"There was a full moon last night," Larisa said. "Vampires always attack on a full moon."

She wasn't kidding. She really thinks Putin is a vampire – Putin and all of Russia.

On Sunday morning, after an attack by 120 rockets and 90 drones that targeted the entire country, fires in power plants and residential buildings had to be extinguished and several cities were completely cut off from mains electricity. Ukraine's telephone networks could barely handle the load as everyone tried to contact their loved ones.

On the Friday before the attack, we had invited a friend to join us at the Sens bookstore on the Khreshchatyk for the presentation of a new book by the Italian chef and populariser of Italian cuisine Marco Cervetti. Our friend did not turn up, but she messaged the next day to explain that she had suffered a minor stroke.

"Is there anything I can do to help?" my wife asked her.

"Kill Putin!" was her curt response. Our friend, like my sister-in-law, was not joking.

Alas, Putin killed more than ten people on Sunday night, including two railway workers. Because of the attack, rail transport in the east and south-east of Ukraine was brought to a halt.

My wife and I spent that terrible night on the train to Mukachevo, in Zakarpattia. At six in the morning, the train stopped in the small town of Stryi, between Lviv and the Carpathian Mountains. We remained there a long time, then moved on to the village of Pavshyno – in the mountains – where the train made an unscheduled stop. I went online and saw that Russian missiles had detonated nearby.

Once we reached Mukachevo, there was nothing to do but sit down in a café and read the details of that night's destruction – the death toll and the number of injured. Interestingly, none of the reports mentioned the new political context in which this mass shelling of Ukraine took place.

Biden is still in charge of the White House, but Trump and his team are already trying to influence world politics with statements, phone calls and, most likely, other behind-the-scenes activity. Trump promised to end the Russian–Ukrainian war in 24 hours. Nobody will press the stopwatch until the day he takes office, but Trump will need to "prepare" Putin and Zelensky to have any hope of fulfilling his promise of a mutually acceptable peace agreement ready to be signed by January 22, 2025.

Nobody on the planet can be oblivious to the fantastical nature of such a promise. But Trump believes in himself with the force of one of Elon Musk's rockets and we can assume that members of Trump's team are already working 24 hours a day to bring this miracle about. Some of them have no doubt called Putin's people in the Kremlin with specific suggestions and advice on how to end the Russian aggression. Rumours of a conversation between Trump and Putin may be false, but almost certainly there has been contact on some level. We can assume that it was in response to this "reaching out" from the Americans that the main Russian T.V. channels began to broadcast offensive reports about the former and future U.S. First Lady, Melania Trump, featuring half-naked photos from her modelling days.

The mass shelling of Ukraine may have been in response to something else – the phone call from Chancellor Scholz to Putin, which certainly took place and lasted about an hour, though no results have been announced. Perhaps someone from the Kremlin will eventually flee to the U.S. and write a book about it. This was almost the only way the West ever received Kremlin inside information during the Soviet era.

What happens if Trump fails to end the Russian–Ukrainian war in the course of his first day as President or even in the first month? He will probably start by apportioning blame for the lack of agreement. The choice of culprits is limited: it is either Zelensky or Putin, but blaming Putin for undermining the peace process would imply the imposition of new sanctions against Russia and increased military aid to Ukraine. This is at odds with the views of Elon Musk, who has become a key Trump adviser and whose role in the new President's team may be decisive. Musk also seems to have had a positive experience while communicating with Putin and the Russian President may allow Musk to influence his decisions if he sees Musk as a key to influencing U.S. policy in the future.

If Musk convinces Trump that the United States should avoid a deterioration in relations with Russia, then Trump will pronounce President Zelensky the one responsible for undermining the U.S. peace initiative. That will be easy because Zelensky will refuse to consider territorial concessions, and Trump will throw up his hands and say: "I tried, but President Zelensky is against the peace process!"

Putin has long demanded Ukraine's renunciation of Crimea, Donbas and southern Ukraine in return for ending the Russian aggression. President Trump may try to make it look as though these concessions are his plan, but who will be fooled by that? If Zelensky is shown to be the one who disrupted the peace process, the United States will not have to make any difficult political or financial decisions in the future and could even remove Ukraine from its political agenda altogether. In that case, Ukraine's fate will depend on the European Union and other democratic countries which understand that this is a conflict between global authoritarianism and global democracy.

Arriving in Mukachevo, my wife and I listened to the air raid sirens and peered into the faces of passers-by. The locals were angry and did not mince their words about Putin. It was the first time since the start of the war that Russia had attacked this border region.

"How could he?" grumbled the waitress in the café. "He promised not to shoot at his friends!"

Hearing this, I could not hold back a sad smile. The waitress noticed my reaction and, thinking that I did not understand, continued: "Orban agreed with him that Russia would not shell Transcarpathia. They are friends!"

Was the attack on the western border region, where many ethnic Hungarians live, an indication that the friendship between Putin and Orban is over? If that friendship is cooling, then the number of dissatisfied residents of Transcarpathia, such as the waitress, will increase sharply. Until yesterday Transcarpathia was considered the safest region in the country. After February 2022, Ukrainians who could afford it bought apartments and houses here, and hundreds of thousands of Ukrainians have moved to the region in the hope of surviving on this "island of safety". Many businesses have transferred production here, away from the regularly shelled central and eastern regions. Where should they go now?

Hungarian Prime Minister Orban has not yet made a statement regarding the shelling of Transcarpathia. We might not expect "Putin's friend" to criticise his actions. Perhaps, however, Orban's recent visit to the U.S., during which Trump called him his main European friend, has affected the way Putin sees Orban. The Hungarian Prime Minister has become a "servant of two masters", and these masters have major grievances against each other.

Was Russia's shelling of Transcarpathia a signal to Orban about the end of the Hungarian–Russian friendship? If the region is targeted in future attacks, we can assume that Putin has crossed Orban off his list of friends – a short list which includes the leaders of North Korea, Iran, Venezuela and perhaps Slovakia. At the bottom, in pencil, we might see the Chinese leader's name. Xi Jinping will soon have to make difficult decisions in communication with the new U.S. President. He may need to decide what is more important for the Chinese economy: the Russian market for drones and cars or the American market for all other goods.

The one positive piece of news that we read while we sat in the Mukachevo café was that Biden had finally allowed Ukraine to use U.S. weapons to target sites inside Russia. We nearly cheered. Yes, this is good news, but we know the risks. Putin must be foaming at the mouth and who knows what an angry vampire will do?

Just in case, I checked the lunar calendar. The next full moon will be on December 15, but that probably won't be as bad as the one on January 25 which is called the "Wolf Moon". I assume we should not expect anything good from Russia on that day. The Wolf Moon, moreover, will rise in the sky on the fifth day after Donald Trump takes office as President of the United States.

19.11.2024

One Thousand Days

As the winter sets in, Russia is once more destroying the remains of Ukraine's energy system, trying to freeze Ukrainians into submission.

In the east of the country, the Russian army is slowly advancing, occupying more and more Ukrainian territory. Their losses are huge, but Putin seems to have no more regard for his own troops than for Ukrainian soldiers and civilians. The war continues because that is Putin's desire. He is determined to blast a change in the map of the world, removing independent Ukraine forever and forcing everyone to accept his fantasy landscape as reality. Faced with this existential threat, Ukrainians have no choice but to fight on. Few believe in the possibility of an acceptable peace agreement with a vampire.

As the countdown of the second thousand days of this war begins, for the first time Russia has attacked Ukraine with an intercontinental ballistic missile designed for nuclear strikes. The Ukrainian government has not reported the result of the attack, which targeted a major industrial plant in Dnipro. We can only imagine the capabilities of a weapon that is 23 metres long and weighs 1,200 kilograms.

Ukraine defends itself and buries its soldiers and civilians every day, hoping that regimes which have no regard for democracy or human rights will be prevented by the U.S. and Europe from dictating the world order in which our children will live.

04.12.2024

Feeling Our Way to the End of the Year

A thick fog hangs over Kyiv and over all of central Ukraine. The humid and heavy air kills visibility. Even on a good, straight road, you must drive at minimum speed. The same thick fog is enveloping Ukraine's immediate military and political prospects. While future President Donald Trump is threatening Hamas and demanding the release of Israeli hostages, the Ukrainian Foreign Ministry has declared its refusal to accept guarantees from N.A.T.O. allies if they are offered in lieu of full N.A.T.O. membership.

It must be obvious to everyone that N.A.T.O. is not seriously considering inviting Ukraine to its military and political alliance in the immediate future. Preventing an escalation in the conflict with Russia remains N.A.T.O.'s priority and the block is pinning its hopes for an end to the conflict on negotiations between Zelensky and Putin. The Foreign Ministry's statement sounded like an ultimatum, but it was not made by President Zelensky, who can avoid responsibility for it and, if needs be, replace the Minister of Foreign Affairs. As we approach January 20 and Donald Trump's arrival in the White House, all military and political processes in Ukraine have gone into overdrive, but, as if it were happening in the foggy air that hangs over the country, this activity is perceived as the indistinct flailing-about of many parties.

Only the Ukrainian Foreign Ministry's statement was clear,

and it was timed to coincide with the meeting of N.A.T.O. foreign ministers in Brussels, where participants preferred to discuss the continuation of military aid to Ukraine rather than Ukraine's accession to the military alliance.

Information flashed through the Ukrainian media that Germany is ready to discuss partial N.A.T.O. membership of Ukraine – membership of part of the country, such as the western regions, while southern and eastern Ukraine remain under the control of Russian troops. These rumours were not discussed at the N.A.T.O. meeting – at least not publicly – but for Ukrainians, they were amplified by the unexpected visit to Ukraine by German Chancellor Olaf Scholz. N.A.T.O. Secretary General Mark Rutte, on the other hand, did mention that Ukraine's path to N.A.T.O. membership requires the signing of bilateral security agreements with each member country of the military alliance – a long and problematic process. It seems extremely unlikely that such an agreement could be signed with Hungary while Viktor Orban is the Prime Minister, or with Slovakia while Robert Fico heads their government.

*

Through the fog of uncertainty, new activity is visible in Ukraine's domestic political life. A convoy of identical, gleaming Mini Cooper cars drove by Kyiv City Hall – a building that has long sported a banner calling on Russia to release Ukrainian prisoners of war, especially the soldiers of the Azov Battalion captured two years ago in Mariupol. Leaning out of the cars were young men with cardboard boxes containing signed demands that the Ukrainian prisoners of war be released.

Why did these activists choose to demonstrate in front of Kyiv City Hall? The Mayor's Office does not deal with prisoner-of-war issues and everyone understands that Russia is responsible for delaying the process. Most likely, what lies behind this eye-catching protest is the long-standing conflict between Kyiv Mayor Vitali Klitschko and the office of President Zelensky. The polished look of the protest indicates that it was orchestrated by some specialists from show business with connections in car dealership circles. In addition, the rally participants appeared to have no fear of being seized by enlistment officers, who, with renewed vigour, have recently been stopping cars with male drivers or passengers.

The Ukrainian Parliament has also seen a revival of activity. The well-known Ukrainian politician – head of the Batkivshchyna party – Yulia Tymoshenko has relaunched herself into public life. While social networks are trying to spread her new "combat" image, she has announced the start of a campaign against Ukraine's pharmaceutical "mafia". She promises to continue her fight until the prices of drugs drop by 200 or 300 per cent. In her video monologues, Tymoshenko compares prices in Polish and Ukrainian pharmacies and says that she will report on each phase of her war against price rigging in Ukraine's pharmaceutical industry.

Medicines are expensive in Ukraine and demand for them is highest among pensioners – a key group of potential pro-Tymoshenko voters, although the M.P.'s current ratings are low. Tymoshenko, who has long dreamed of becoming President, seems to have decided to draw some attention to herself, reminding voters that she is still in Parliament and still defending the interests of Ukrainian people.

Ukrainians, meanwhile, are simultaneously discussing tax increases and the 1,000-hryvnia (£19 at March 2025) "winter support" gift that President Zelensky is offering every Ukrainian who is in the country. To receive your 1,000 hryvnias, you need to submit an electronic application or fill out a paper application at the post office.

In 2008, as Prime Minister, Yulia Tymoshenko also gave 1,000 hryvnias to those citizens who had lost their savings during the collapse of the Soviet Union. At that time, the handout was equal to about £134. The pro-Russian President Viktor Yanukovych, who fled to Moscow during the Euromaidan in 2014, also had a 1,000-hryvnia handout to Ukrainians in his 2012 programme. In 2012, the sum was equal to about £77. If nothing else, we can use these handouts to track the depreciation of Ukraine's currency.

Food prices have risen steeply since the summer, and in early December the government raised taxes on businesses and increased the temporary "army tax" – paid on all earned income – from 1.5 per cent. to 5 per cent. Many see "Zelensky's thousand" as a form of compensation for the tax hike. The beginning of December may be the best time for tax increases and other unpleasant innovations because a person has a choice: to think about the new problems or to allow themselves to be distracted by thoughts of the upcoming festivities. The mood of most Ukrainians is not at all festive. It is, however, almost impossible not to think about Christmas and the new year, especially if there are children in the family. In our nearest supermarket, boxes of Christmas sweets are already being sold at discounted prices. I don't remember this happening before.

In Kyiv and other cities, Christmas trees have been set up in the central squares. Children's theatres are preparing festive performances. Winter skating rinks and skate rental points are opening.

The office party season is also under way but employees are afraid that uninvited guests from the enlistment office could gatecrash the festivities. Ukrainians are creative and always ready with non-standard solutions to challenges. To avoid unwanted attention, corporate events will perhaps take place at unusual venues – on the territory of a military unit, for example, or in the workshop of a munitions plant.

This year, creativity has reached new heights among Ukraine's criminal elements. In Cherkasy region, in the centre of Ukraine, prominent representatives of the country's criminal elite organised a get-together on the territory of a penitentiary. The meeting was attended by three inmates and several of their esteemed colleagues who were at large at the time. The director of the prison who allowed this gathering to take place inside the colony is under arrest and awaiting trial, as are the party guests.

As the end of the year approaches, the government is seeking ways to strengthen its domestic policies and has renamed the Ministry for the Integration of the Occupied Territories. It is now the Ministry of National Unity. At its head will be Oleksiy Chernyshev, former head of the board of the national oil company Naftogaz.

"The creation of the Ministry of National Unity will contribute to the formation of a strategy on how to ensure that Ukrainians return to live and work in Ukraine," explained Prime Minister Denys Shmyhal.

The mass return of Ukrainian refugees will only be possible once the war ends and we see a stable peace guaranteed by N.A.T.O. member countries. Everyone understands this, including Ukrainian politicians who remember the Budapest Memorandum with its assurances of the inviolability of Ukrainian territory in exchange for Ukraine's surrender of nuclear weapons. It was signed in Budapest exactly 30 years ago, on December 5, 1994, when Russia, the United States and Great Britain gave assurances of the security and inviolability of Ukrainian borders.

Today, N.A.T.O. is looking for new forms of "assurances" that will encourage President Zelensky to sit down at the negotiation table with Putin. It is interesting that for their last meeting of the year, the N.A.T.O. foreign ministers chose a date that practically coincides with the anniversary of one of modern history's greatest geopolitical deceptions: the impotent Budapest Memorandum.

17.12.2024

Naive Art and Sobering Reality

As we approach the holiday season, Ukraine's cultural life, always colourful, has become ever more vibrant. A Christmas tree has been put up in Kyiv's Sophia Square by order of the Mayor. It is half the size of last year's and it is not a real, green tree, but a shiny white one – as if some terrible shock had taken the colour from its branches. Sell-out premières of lively shows are on at the theatres and posters advertising gala performances of popular stand-up comedians and pop singers are on display all over the city. Kyiv is trying to distract itself from reality and, deciding to support this trend, I went to the Ukrainian House cultural centre to see an exhibition of Ukrainian naive art: "Naive Free".

I expected a small exhibition centred around the best-known Ukrainian artist of the genre, Maria Primachenko, who achieved renown in the 1960s. The museum near Kyiv dedicated to her work was destroyed by a Russian missile at the very beginning of the war. Fortunately, many of the paintings were rescued, and the attack increased the symbolic and commercial value of her work.

The "Naive Free" exhibition was very different from what I expected. Focusing on works from the 19th and 20th centuries, it shows that the tradition of naive art in Ukraine is far older and richer than you might think. Hundreds of fascinating works from all over the country kept me entertained for more than two hours and I left only very reluctantly.

Although naive art is rightly associated with the "professional" naivety of the amateur artist and with his or her perception of the world, it is not exclusively non-violent. There were scenes of "farewell" to the tsarist army in the exhibition, but I missed examples of the naive art created during the last three years which reflect our new reality, including the reality at the front line. The absence of works by Primachenko did not upset me at all. Not long ago, a large exhibition of her paintings was held in Kyiv and Ukrainians know her paintings "by heart", especially the fantastic and colourful animals that she created.

At the beginning of the war, one of Primachenko's works – "Flowers that grew near the fourth Chernobyl power block" – was sold for half a million dollars at a charity auction in aid of the Ukrainian army. This work was saved from the ashes of the Primachenko museum and the money bought 125 second-hand jeeps, pickups and minibuses for the front. Later, Ukrainian collectors of naive paintings donated several more of her works for similar charity auctions. From beyond the grave, Primachenko is sponsoring the army – an active participant in Ukraine's struggle against its enemy.

Russian aggression has encouraged Ukrainians consciously or subconsciously to adopt Primachenko's works as a means of protecting and strengthening their national identity. Her magical animals have become a popular "commodity", used to indicate affiliation to the cause. In expensive, made-in-Ukraine boutiques you can buy everything from jewellery to T-shirts featuring these motifs. Ukrainian naive art seems to have become more powerful than professional artistic creativity.

The "Naive Free" exhibition made me think about the key addressee of naive art: the "ordinary" people who make up 90 per cent. of any society. Naivety, especially regarding political and economic matters, would figure quite high on a list of qualities used to describe "the average Ukrainian", if such a person can be imagined. But it would also figure in descriptions of people in neighbouring countries, where political naivety has helped to bring populists to power.

Naivety makes Ukrainians easy victims of scams. In the early 2000s, "financial pyramids" relieved a good many people of their life savings. Today the danger comes from telephone fraud. Every few days I receive text messages saying that financial assistance has been allocated to me by the state or that the U.N. is giving me 1,000€: "You only need to complete an online form to receive the money!" I recognise these scams immediately, but I see the fraudsters growing cleverer by the day, and I wonder when I may be tempted to make that fatal click.

Getting justice for victims of this type of fraud is an almost impossible task. While the police are busy helping the military enlistment officers check the documents of potential servicemen on the streets, in bars and at rock concerts, the number of telephone scammers is increasing. There are powerful call centres with dozens of "employees" who receive a basic salary from their criminal bosses, plus a percentage of the money they succeed in stealing from their victims' bank accounts. Sometimes the police manage to find one of these call centres and arrests are made. The current shortage of judges, however, means that the courts have a huge backlog of cases. Early next year, we will see an attempt to resolve this problem with the launch of the largest competitive recruitment drive in the history of independent Ukraine. Vacancies for 1,800 judges will be advertised.

While this recruitment campaign may help to bring more scammers to justice, I am not sure it will help in the fight against naivety. There is, on the other hand, one group that shows no sign of this characteristic: the Ukrainian military. They understand how serious and dangerous the current situation is and regularly report about it, not only to their commanders and the country's leadership but also to ordinary Ukrainians via instant messengers and YouTube channels. Their comments have a sobering effect – much like a cold shower – but they also provoke many Ukrainians to increase their faith in miracles, like the one they believe Trump will perform immediately after his election.

Sincerely, or otherwise, some Ukrainian officials support this "faith in miracles". The head of the Odesa Regional Military Administration, Oleg Kiper, recently announced that, at the beginning of the full-scale war, Odesa was saved from the Russian army by the Odesa Metropolitan Agathangel – the head of the Ukrainian Orthodox Church of the Moscow Patriarchate. During the first days of the Russian invasion, Agathangel travelled along the entire coast of Odesa region holding an icon that is said to possess miraculous powers. Indeed, a storm raged off the coast for a full ten days, preventing the Russian navy from landing troops. Was it a miracle? In a sense, it was. But can the

Church of the Moscow Patriarchate claim this miracle as their own? Surely it is just one of thousands of miracles that, on a daily basis, allow Ukraine to go on defending itself from Russia.

We do not know what miracles 2025 will bring, but I am sure that, with all its problems and achievements, losses and victories, Ukraine will enter the new year and continue the struggle with the same dogged determination and with many Ukrainians clinging to the hope of further miracles.

Perhaps it is this seemingly naive stubbornness that lies at the heart of Ukrainian invincibility: the inexhaustible readiness to rise from yet another layer of ashes in a blaze of colour, like the paintings of Maria Primachenko.

31.12.2024

Hope

As Christmas and the new year approach, the mood of Ukrainians has improved a little. The end of the year brings hope of something new, and the overwhelming majority of Ukrainians are united by one particular hope. While children wait for their New Year presents, adults are waiting for the war to stop. We are not expecting victory – or even a complete cessation of hostilities. We are hoping for Donald Trump to fulfil the promise he made during his presidential campaign: to stop the war. Many Ukrainians desperately want to believe that he will succeed. What remains unclear are the conditions under which this war can be stopped and how long that "stop" will hold.

Sadly, I belong to that group of Ukrainians who believe that a real end to the war is possible only after the death of Vladimir Putin. As long as he is alive, the war will continue. After all, this is the last war in his life, and he wants to emerge victorious. He has already chiselled his victory into the stone of the Russian constitution, forcing Parliament – the State Duma – to inscribe bits of Ukrainian territory into the constitution, including areas currently under the control of the Ukrainian government. Does anyone really think that some negotiations with Trump will lead to the reversal of those changes and the "return" of Ukrainian lands to their rightful owner?

The amendment to the Russian constitution is a time bomb that is very difficult, if not impossible, to defuse. As things stand, I see only one circumstance that could lead to a lasting peace between Russia and Ukraine: if, after Putin's demise (as happened in the case of Khrushchev after Stalin's death), someone comes to power in Russia who declares that the previous ruler was a criminal.

In November, after Trump's victory in the presidential election, the mood of Ukrainians was gloomy, but within only a few weeks, a wonderful metamorphosis occurred. As Trump began to hold forth during interviews and speeches about achieving a just peace in the region, we started to believe that the President-Elect understood the issues involved and meant what he was saying. America has always advocated for the principle of justice, although it has not always adhered to this principle in its foreign policy. After a short meeting between Trump and Zelensky, even officials in the Ukrainian presidential administration started to believe in Trump's ability to achieve peace. In at least one of his recent speeches, President Zelensky himself said that if Trump can stop the war in one day, then perhaps Ukraine can be accepted into the European Union and N.A.T.O. in one day. Some people thought Zelensky was being ironic, while others heard in his words a message for the European and N.A.T.O. leadership: "Be like Trump! Be categorical and decisive!"

In the meantime, we live our lives to the sounds of exploding missiles and drones, to the whistle of shrapnel and the ringing of broken glass. Every time a siren sounds in Kyiv, we check our phones to find out the reason behind the alert.

If a drone attack is expected, people tend not to react any more. Despite evidence to the contrary, they believe that the air defence forces around the capital will be able to shoot down the drones which have petrol engines and can only fly at relatively low speeds. If the threat is from ballistic or cruise missiles, on the other hand, citizens take the air raid warning more seriously. A new threat – a medium-range missile with multiple warheads called the Oreshnik – has recently appeared. If we hear that one of those is heading our way, we are more likely to go to the metro station, taking the escalator down to a safe depth. Every day, it seems, the number and type of dangers lying in wait for Ukraine's civilian population increases. In 2024, as well as the Oreshnik missile, soldiers from North Korea were added to the list of threats we face, but it seems unlikely that Putin will be able to frighten us in 2025 more than he has this year. Of course, he has nuclear weapons in reserve, but Russian politicians – including the President himself – have threatened us with such weapons so often that most Ukrainians are simply tired of thinking about it.

We are tired of thinking about danger in general. I remember my emotions when a Russian missile hit Kyiv's main children's hospital in July. I went home from the café where I had been working to find that my younger son and his friend had gone to the bomb site to help clear the rubble. I could not work any more that day. I waited for my son to return, knowing that Russia likes to hit the same target twice – to kill those who are helping the victims of the first attack. There was no second strike on the hospital, but the 38 missiles fired by Russia at Kyiv on that day killed 33 people, including five children. That day will forever remain in my memory.

The best moment of the year occurred only ten days before that blast, when the Crimean Tatar leader, Nariman Dzhelyal, was freed from Russian imprisonment as part of a prisoner exchange. We met a few days later in "Yalta", a Crimean Tatar restaurant in the centre of Kyiv. I was amazed and heartened by his energy and positive spirit. Dzhelyal's wife and children left Crimea to join him in Kyiv. Like all internally displaced people from the peninsula, they dream of going home, but for now Zelensky has made Dzhelyal Ukrainian Ambassador to Türkiye, where there is a very large Crimean Tatar population.

This year, Ukraine's last "island of security" – an area that had not been targeted by Russian missiles – disappeared. For almost three years, the region of Transcarpathia, which borders Hungary, Romania and Slovakia, was considered the safest region of Ukraine because of the pro-Russian sympathies of Hungarian Prime Minister Viktor Orban. More than 200,000 ethnic Hungarians live in the region and Ukrainians assume that it was left in peace because Orban requested this of Putin. In the past two months, however, Russian missiles have regularly targeted the area. The power lines which connect the Ukrainian energy system with the European one pass through this region. This power "highway" allows Europe to supply Ukraine with electricity when the country has been plunged into darkness by Russian attacks on Ukrainian power plants. We can only pray that the power lines remain intact.

Our enemy is doing everything it can to crush us: North

Korean trains with missile launchers and other military equipment enter Russian territory. There the equipment is reloaded onto Russian trains and sent west, towards the front. South Korean intelligence has warned that their northern neighbour is preparing a new wave of soldiers to fight Ukraine and that Pyongyang is mass-producing attack drones for export to Russia.

Russian troops are actively preparing to storm the cities of Kherson and Zaporizhzhia, which are already included in the Constitution of the Russian Federation as part of its territory. As if all that was not grotesque enough, in contravention of the Russian Constitution, the Spiritual Administration of Muslims in Russia, which is under the control of the Kremlin, has granted permission to Russian Muslim men to have up to four wives. The Russian army needs soldiers and allowing polygamy may help to provide them, although no bill on the legalisation of polygamy has been submitted to the State Duma. At the same time, a bill concerning other lifestyle choices has been submitted to the State Duma and it aims to place a ban on propaganda supporting "a selfish, consumerist or isolated lifestyle". According to the Russian M.P. Olga Borisova, the desire to be "on your own" is the main threat to Russian traditional family values. This bill will be considered in the near future.

So as Russia revs up to continue the war at full blast, Ukraine is still waiting for a miracle from Trump. With the longest night of the year behind us, many Ukrainians are pinning their hopes on the coming of spring (Putin can't control the seasons!) and with it, peace.

Back in November, my wife planted many daffodil and

tulip bulbs around our village house. We will plant more vegetables when the earth warms up in the spring.

Although we have a village house and garden, I remain a city dweller at heart. I see in both rural and urban communities the same steadfastness. We won't have our lives turned upside down by war. We stay and simply adapt our habits and lifestyle to the wartime situation. We know where the nearest bomb shelters are. We go to restaurants and cafés more than ever – perhaps because we want every day to be a small holiday or want to support any business that is still functioning in these difficult conditions. We are in a hurry to get even a tiny dose of pleasure and happiness. Tomorrow the restaurant may no longer exist – it could be blown up by a Russian missile, like the one that destroyed the Azerbaijani restaurant ShakhPlov on Antonovycha Street a couple of days ago. I am sorry we never got to eat there.

Like most Ukrainians today, we live one day at a time and are happy each morning when we wake up in one piece. It would be disingenuous to say that I don't believe in New Year miracles or the President Trump "miracle". I await his inauguration on January 20 with much more impatience than I awaited the turn of the century twenty-five years ago. What great expectations we had of this century and the changes it would bring to all our lives!

01.01.2025

Fast away the Old Year Passes . . .

The old year passes, taking with it people you will never meet again, some more familiar, some less. The stroke of midnight brushes into the past all the events of the previous twelve months: weddings, anniversaries, sports competitions and official state visits. In wartime, the old year carries away much more than a peacetime year can. It consigns to history factories, farms, museums, theatres and hospitals. It sweeps away entire cities into the irretrievable past. Maryinka in Donetsk region was destroyed by Russian shelling. No-one lives there now. Many other towns and villages met the same fate during 2024.

Last year turned into a slow farewell to the once-flourishing city of Pokrovsk in the west of Donetsk region. Trains were still going there in the summer. In September, when banks and shops began to close, Pokrovsk had about 30,000 residents – half of its pre-war population.

On September 27, the last evacuation train drew out of the city. While Russia continued to bomb and shell Pokrovsk, the most stubborn residents refused to believe that the same thing would happen to their hometown as had happened to Chasiv Yar and many other settlements in Donbas: slow but sure destruction. At that time, Russian troops were ten kilometres away. Today they are right at the edge of the city and, at night, small groups try to break through into Pokrovsk proper where 7,500 people are still hiding, trying to survive in partially destroyed buildings. The trauma they have suffered has made them impervious to suggestions that they should leave. How do they live in a city that no longer exists?

How do they survive without windows or heating? Some day, books and films about this will appear and audiences will empathise with the heroes of the stories and wipe away tears – pained by the memory of this tragedy. But today this is not a memory. It is happening as I write, and it is just one of thousands of tragedies caused by the Russian war. The story of Pokrovsk is dramatic, but it is only part of a huge tableau called "Aggression".

In the ruins of the city, in addition to the 7,500 residents, there are Ukrainian soldiers who daily engage in battle with the Russian army. We are no longer talking about protecting a city – it is now only "territory", Ukrainian territory. The city practically no longer exists. Abandoned cats and dogs search for food in the rubble. Volunteers are still risking their lives to reach Pokrovsk and evacuate the animals.

The Russian army has suffered huge losses in manpower and equipment in their attempts to take Pokrovsk, but it seems its leaders have decided to simply bypass the ruins without engaging in any further direct battles. They want to cut off the Ukrainian army's supply routes – to encircle Pokrovsk, trapping the remaining inhabitants – and move on to Sloviansk and Kramatorsk.

In December 2024 a monument to Ukraine's national poet Taras Shevchenko and a coffin containing the body of Danilo Shumuk, a veteran of the struggle for Ukrainian independence who died in Pokrovsk in 2004, were removed from the city. The monument to Shevchenko has been taken to the town of Samar in Dnipropetrovsk region. Danilo Shumuk's body was reburied at the Likhachev Cemetery in Lviv. The Ukrainian military organised the reinterment, confident that when the Russians occupy the ruins of Pokrovsk, they will destroy the graves of any anti-Soviet activists. Shumuk spent almost 30 years in prisons and concentration camps. Some of his descendants – captured Ukrainian soldiers, accused of terrorist activities – are languishing in the same prisons and camps.

The end of 2024 was dramatic for Ukraine not only because of events on the front line. Ten days before the new year, Russia's cyber-terrorists carried out their largest and, it must be admitted, most effective attack on Ukrainian government data systems, destroying state electronic registers of real estate, business and civil status acts as well as many other databases. This sabotage has not returned Ukraine to the Stone Age, but it has directed us back to pen and paper. Births, deaths and marriages are being recorded in hard copy so that when the electronic registers are restored, the information can be transferred to the "state data cloud".

The attack has brought a halt to all real-estate transactions. It is still unclear whether back-up copies of the registers were damaged and whether data was interfered with in any way. For the current government, this cyber-attack was especially painful. President Zelensky and his team were proud of their digitalisation strategy. Launched in 2019, most Ukrainian citizens were persuaded to install in their smartphones the Diya application, which is directly linked to almost all government services. "Electronic public administration" was President Zelensky's greatest achievement before Russia's full-scale invasion.

It is not clear whether Russia planned the cyberattack as a New Year "gift" to Ukraine, or whether the timing was accidental, but the approach of the festive season initially softened the blow. After three days of frenzied discussion about the damage done by the attack, Ukrainians decided to wait patiently for the system to be restored. The government promised that the registers and databases would be available again in two weeks and we all want to believe that. The registers contain records of real estate in annexed Crimea and the occupied territories of Donbas. The details of property, both private and state, that has been destroyed by Russian bombs are also recorded in these registers. They will be required to calculate reparation payments that will one day be imposed on the Russian Federation. According to preliminary estimates, since February 2022, Russia has destroyed the residential property of 3.5 million Ukrainians.

Russia has been firing bombs at homes in its own Kursk region since last summer in an attempt to dislodge the Ukrainian expeditionary force. On social networks, Kursk residents have posted tearful video appeals to President Putin, asking for compensation for lost housing, money to rent other accommodation and for I.D.P. or refugee status so that they can receive regular financial assistance. In response, the Russian government has agreed to make a one-off payment of between $750 and $1,500 for each damaged or destroyed home. It was announced that certificates for square metres of new housing would be issued, but there is confusion about how to obtain these certificates and doubts as to whether they will materialise at all. "Every shell costs money!" the new governor of the region, Alexander Khinshtein, told residents. "The state will not compensate 100 per cent. of the costs." Yes, the Russian government's priority is the production of missiles and bombs used primarily to destroy Ukrainian homes and infrastructure.

Before the new year, Ukrainians debated funding for festivities. Some citizens spoke out against the installation of Christmas trees and decorations in city centres, demanding that local authorities transfer all funds budgeted for such purposes to the Ukrainian army and defence industry. In many large cities, however, the "pro-Christmas decorations" lobby won. On Kyiv's Sophia Square, the tree was rather small and very plastic. Kharkiv, on the other hand, treated its residents to three luxuriously large trees with spots set up for photo opportunities. True, they were all installed underground, where Russian bombs and missiles could not reach – in the Universytet, Nauchnaya and Istorychnyi Myzei metro stations. A St Nicholas grotto was opened at the Istorychnyi Myzei station with a mailbox for children's letters to St Nick. There were concerts on the platform throughout the Christmas period and tens of thousands of families went underground to enjoy the celebrations.

While Ukrainian parents were distracting their children from the war with festive treats, a video was shown on Russian television in which air defences shoot down a sleigh carrying Santa Claus and pulled across the skies above Moscow by six reindeer. The video's catchphrase was: "We don't need anything foreign in our skies!" I am sure that you will find similar phrases in the Ukrainian children's letters to St Nicholas: "We don't need anything Russian in our skies!"

Russia, of course, is not only killing Ukrainians, as was demonstrated by the shooting down of the Azerbaijani plane on Christmas Day. The reverberation from that tragedy and Russia's cyberattack on Ukraine will be felt far into the new year.

06.01.2025

Two Empty Seats

On the evening of January 1, 2025, Kyiv's Ivan Franko Drama Theatre performed the classic Ukrainian vaudeville piece "Natalka Poltavka". Tickets were sold out, but two seats in the second row, right in front of the stage, remained unoccupied. Seats 25 and 26 had been bought by a married couple, professors at Shevchenko University, Igor Zima and Lesya Sokur. They were planning to greet the new year with a trip to the theatre, which was only a five-minute walk from their apartment. Alas, on New Year's morning, a Russian drone struck their home on the top floor of a beautiful, turreted building in Kyiv's government quarter. The apartment no longer exists. The owners were killed instantly and were buried in Baikove Cemetery a few days ago.

The drone explosion that killed the couple partially destroyed the apartment on the floor below, whose owner, a well-known politician, had planned to rent it out. One floor further down lives Lyudmila Meshkova – the 86-year-old grand dame of Kyiv's fine art world who created a style of painting on ceramics. Her works hang in the U.N.E.S.C.O. headquarters in Paris and in the White House. Caring activists are raising money to help her repair the damage to her apartment. Unfortunately, it will be difficult to organise the renovation work. Conscription has left few builders available and the apartment's location will cause other problems. The building is 200 metres from the Office of the President and only 100 metres from the National Bank. Since 2022 the area has been blocked by military checkpoints. Only residents or people with special passes can enter. This is the first time a Russian drone has penetrated this heavily defended quarter and the fact that it happened on New Year's Day does not bode well for 2025.

Kyiv had been left relatively undisturbed over Christmas, and one of the events my wife and I were able to enjoy took place at the Art Mall, on the southern edge of Kyiv, which houses an excellent gallery of contemporary Ukrainian art. On the evening we visited the gallery there was an auction to raise money for the army and a wonderful performance of Ukrainian carols by the early music ensemble Chorea Kozacka. The art and music had us feeling inspired, but as we left for home, an air raid siren sounded. I tried to book an Uber, but having entered my destination in the app, I received a strange message: "Unfortunately, Uber is not available in your country." I tried again and got the same response. Confused, I opened the G.P.S. map and clicked on the icon showing my current coordinates. A thick blue dot appeared on the map at my location: "32 Lenin Street, Mozyr, Belarus".

A middle-aged man standing by the roadside near us sighed as he put away his phone.

"Are you in Belarus too?" he said. "It's G.P.S. interference. They do it to confuse Russia's Iranian drones!"

We did not hear any explosions that evening. Perhaps it was thanks to the electronic defence systems which are able to disorientate Russian drones and redirect them out of Ukraine. "Our cyber soldiers must have to be very careful with their redirection tricks," I thought to myself as we walked to the metro station. "Poland is very close. We wouldn't want a Russian drone to land there."

*

Poland is one of our staunchest allies despite some longstanding differences which a group of Polish and Ukrainian historians have been trying to resolve. In Ukraine, the thorny issue that stands between us and our Polish neighbours is called the "Volyn tragedy" – events that took place in the Volyn region which borders Poland and Belarus.

Before the Second World War, tens of thousands of Poles lived in Volyn alongside Ukrainians. On Sunday, July 11, 1943, when both Ukraine and Poland were occupied by Nazi Germany, fighters from the Organisation of Ukrainian Nationalists and the Ukrainian Insurgent Army carried out coordinated attacks on more than a hundred Polish villages and hamlets, killing about 8,000 Polish residents, including women, children and the elderly.

In Polish that day is known as "Bloody Sunday" and in 2016, the Polish Parliament decided to mark it as the National Day of Remembrance of the Victims of Genocide.

Attacks by Ukrainians on Poles and by Poles on Ukrainians in Volyn began earlier and did not end on "Bloody Sunday". In total, about 60,000 Poles and up to 3,000 Ukrainians died during the "Volyn massacre" (1942–3), as these events are referred to in Poland. The figures are not exact because only 5 per cent. of the Polish victims' burial sites have been discovered.

In mid-December, fourteen Polish and ten Ukrainian historians signed a communiqué which speaks with a more decisive and pragmatic voice than politicians have hitherto used when addressing this painful topic. The authors of the communiqué called on Ukrainians and Poles to "accept the paradigm of all victims are our victims", to refuse to divide the victims of the "Volyn massacre" into "ours" and "theirs" and to refuse to use the "Volyn massacre" for political purposes because that only leads to increased contention between Poland and Ukraine.

The historians propose, instead, to begin exhuming the unmarked mass graves so as to create cemeteries and necropolises, to condemn all acts of vandalism against the burial sites and to restore previously destroyed notices and monuments to the victims of Ukrainian–Polish hostility, both on the territory of Ukraine and on the territory of Poland, where about 8,000 Ukrainians fell victim to the Poles.

The text of the communiqué is the result of an extensive study by the joint group, which considered not only the events in Volyn, but also disagreements between the two countries regarding the assessment of other dramatic events in the periods between 1917 and 1923, and 1937 and 1947.

Complete mutual understanding with Poland is certainly in Ukraine's interests. Following the publication of the communiqué, however, the Ukrainian signatories came under intense criticism from some compatriots who accused them of "surrendering national interests".

This pressure caused two Ukrainian historians to withdraw their signatures, but among those who did not withdraw was Yaroslav Hrytsak, Professor of the Ukrainian Catholic

University in Lviv and one of Ukraine's best-known historians, who said: "Signing [the communiqué] means that we are ready to talk to each other . . . We do not want the Volyn Case to become the main topic in Poland's presidential election." Hrytsak is right. The first round of the Polish presidential elections will take place in just four months, on May 18. The topic of the "Volyn massacre", or "Volyn tragedy", is bound to come up and could influence the outcome of the elections.

The Ukrainian government has at last lifted the ban on the exhumation of Polish mass graves in Ukraine, and the vital process of discovering and honouring the victims of the events of 1942–3 has begun. In western Belarus, meanwhile, a campaign to destroy the burial sites of Polish soldiers and memorials related to the Polish history of the territory has been going on for two years. Sometimes monuments and burial sites are demolished on the orders of local authorities, sometimes the destruction is passed off as acts of vandalism. Polish–Belarusian relations are currently frozen. Against this backdrop, from the high ground of the new year, one can look at the future of Polish–Ukrainian relations with cautious optimism.

We can all be grateful to the historians for grappling with this complex and sensitive task. I also thank Ukraine's talented cyber soldiers whose efforts save lives every day. It is only very sad that they were not able to redirect the drone that landed in Kyiv's government district on January 1, leaving two seats empty at the Ivan Franko Drama Theatre.

19.01.2025

The Dnipro at War

It is a leisurely 25-minute walk to the Dnipro River from my home in Kyiv's "top town" – the 1,000-year-old hilltop fortress-city, accessed from the south via the Golden Gate. But to get down to the river, I need to walk south-east, passing under the white walls of the St Sophia Monastery, with its majestic 11th-century cathedral, and head towards St Andrew's Church, perched on the edge of the hill above Podil – the old artisan and trading district which is connected to the top town by Kyiv's favourite street, Andriivsky Descent.

As you navigate this steep, cobblestoned ravine, you feel like rainwater rushing down to the river, to the Dnipro. On a sunny day, Andriivsky Descent becomes a dried-up stream, twisting around the hill. Only at the very bottom, in the flatness that is Podil, do right angles and straight lines appear, and if you follow the straight line, within ten minutes you are standing by the Dnipro – Ukraine's main artery whose east and west were seamed together and served equally by its mighty flow. I say "were" because in front of you today is a changed river. In front of you is the Dnipro at war.

The river is at war. When the first bombs hit the city in February 2022, its very current seemed to slacken, as if the river needed time to grasp what was happening in the city, to take a closer look at the flashes of rocket explosions and the fires.

The speed of the river's flow has not changed. The Dnipro seems listless for another reason: the absence of peaceful navigation. For three years now, owners of river-ships, motor-boats and yachts have been banned from going out on the water. Amateur fishermen's inflatable dinghies – once a feature of the river – have disappeared. Under martial law they may only fish from the shore. Friends say that in places where the Dnipro is especially wide, where in bad weather it is impossible to see the opposite bank, some fishermen still row out and try to catch a large pikeperch or even a catfish. But the same friends say that there are almost no fish to be had these days, as if they have all dived to an inaccessible depth because of the war – because of the explosions and the constant threat of destruction and death hanging over all of Ukraine. This, of course, sounds like a myth or a scary fairy tale for adults. Yet legends and fairy tales are fitting means to express the significance of great rivers and the lands and people they serve.

The Dnipro is historically considered part of the route "from the Varangians to the Greeks", from Scandinavia to south-eastern Europe. Rivers were indeed the first highways, and during the last three years, the Dnipro has become a highway for the enemy. Russia often programmes the navigation systems of attack drones and missiles to follow the course of the river. It is difficult to intercept a missile or drone flying low over the waters of the widest river in Ukraine. That is why, especially at night, military boats with anti-aircraft guns mounted on their decks patrol the Dnipro. They are hunting the drones trying to sneak all the way to the centre of Kyiv. When anti-aircraft guns shoot at these winged marauders, a powerful echo sounds in all directions: up- and downstream, and over both riverbanks. On the left bank of the Dnipro, eight kilometres from the city, live our friends, who have not slept properly for more than two years. The echo of artillery fire, and especially the explosion of a drone intercepted over the water, rattles all the windows of their house, piercing their dreams. Having a home by the river has lost much of its charm.

I am not a fish. I cannot imagine how artillery fire and explosions are experienced underwater, but I can easily believe that the fish of the Dnipro have swum away, looking for a quieter life. Like them, residents of the towns and villages along the river have left in search of safety in the west of Ukraine or abroad. Of the Kyivites who became refugees at the beginning of the war, however, a good number have returned. They go to stand and stare at the Dnipro, to witness this symbol of eternity, to find evidence that the power of nature is stronger than our enemies. The river is not afraid of war, just as water is not afraid of fire.

The river calmly invites us to emulate its steady flow, to relax. An evening campfire, singing along to a guitar, a barbecue, night-swimming in the warm, August water – these are the romantic moments connected with the Dnipro of so many generations, and they are mine. The traditions were always the same, only the choice of location varied. My friends and I preferred the Hydropark or Trukhaniv Island – the islands most easily accessible from the city centre.

The Hydropark is a place of entertainment. It has a metro station, dozens of cafés and long stretches of clean river sand – enough space for thousands of visitors. Trukhaniv

Island is a wilder place, overgrown with forest, and the beaches and footpaths are lonelier. To reach this island you must traverse a modestly splendid pedestrian suspension bridge. I crossed it hundreds of times as a youngster on my way to the rowing club where I trained. Almost all of Kyiv's watersport centres are hidden on this island. But it is the Hydropark where adventures await. A place of rendezvous with nature and loved ones; you go there to watch what happens to others and eventually something happens to you.

The Hydropark also attracts anarchic entrepreneurs who try to create businesses beyond official boundaries – away from state control and regulations. For over a year I have not been near the ashes of my favourite café: Jungle Cat. I do not know what happened to its owner. I believe he spent his winters in Cambodia and Kyiv's warm months on the right bank of the Hydropark island, busy at his Jungle Cat. For me, he will always be a symbol of unwavering stubbornness and entrepreneurial anarchism. Accusing him of building the café illegally, prosecutors came to him demanding bribes for not demolishing it. I lost track of how many times his Jungle Cat was torn down, but he stubbornly rebuilt it and reopened for business.

The struggle lasted almost twenty years. He must have believed that the island-park belonged to all Kyivites, that it was a territory of total liberty – liberty in the Ukrainian sense of the word which is equal to anarchy. Downstream 280 miles, the Dnipro is home to Ukraine's best-known island of liberty: Khortytsia, which lies within the borders of another large city, Zaporizhzhia. Khortytsia was the training ground and the fortress home of Cossacks who refused to submit to the Russian Tsar.

On the Hydropark island, the Jungle Cat café stood opposite the Kyiv-Pechersk Lavra – Ukraine's most authoritative monastery, which until recently was subordinate to Moscow. At some point, the owner of the café set up two home-made cannons on the shore. Throughout the day, his staff shot fireworks from them in the direction of the Lavra. The café-goers and river tourists were delighted. The blasts were timed to coincide with the passing of pleasure boats which sounded their horns in response, as if saluting the one-man struggle against officialdom – his battle for the right to serve people in his café, the right to his liberty, to his anarchic self.

The Hydropark still lives its own life. There are fewer cafés now, but people still flock to its shores during our wartime summers and on winter mornings lovers of freezing cold water still gather for a dip in the Dnipro. A thick layer of ice is rare these days but in the past it was common to see winter swimmers with axes gouging out holes before jumping in. It was they who gave me the idea that a penguin would find it cosy to swim there. This is how *Death and the Penguin* was born – a novel about 1990s Kyiv in which the Dnipro plays an important role and where the heroes, including Misha the penguin, cross the entire river walking on the ice.

This year, the winter is warm and instead of snow, rain falls on Kyiv. As a child, I dreamed of swimming across the Dnipro. I swam well then, but I never swam across the Dnipro. I remember this unrealised dream with pleasure. I keep the memory as a souvenir of the times when dreams were non-material.

The Dnipro continues to "haunt" my work. In *The President's Last Love*, the main character regularly walks across the pedestrian bridge to Trukhaniv Island to visit an old hermit who has settled there illegally. My new novel is set in Kyiv in 1919, during the civil war. There was no bridge to Trukhaniv Island at that time and Samson, the young police investigator, must cross the water by boat to search for a suspect. In those days, several hundred people lived there. I have found many old photographs of the island settlement. A church towered over the shore and, with no bridge, dozens of boatmen earned a living ferrying residents to and from the city.

Thoughts about Kyiv's past, the life of the Dnipro River and the people who have lived along its banks sometimes distract me from the war. They bolster my spirits, feeding the hope that the war will end and that Ukraine will emerge from it free and with honour.

I go down to the Dnipro less often these days. It may take only twenty-five minutes to reach it, but the way back is longer. It is uphill and I am getting older. The park on Vladimirskiy Hill is only a ten-minute walk from my home. It hangs above the river and allows you to watch the Dnipro without going down to it. Sometimes I walk there, near the monument to Prince Vladimir the Great – boarded up against shelling. I watch the river and the people who, like me, stand to admire from above its broad, silver ribbon.

I would very much like to see ships, barges and yachts going up and down again. But they will not appear until the war ends. They are in the secret bays near Kyiv, hiding among the river's many small islands. They are waiting for the end of the war, waiting to sail this great river once more. Like the Ukrainian refugees in Europe, they wait to return to their berths along the Dnipro's shores.

28.01.2025

A Tale of Two Machos

Less than two weeks have passed since Donald Trump took office, but the world is reeling from the new geopolitical conflicts provoked by the 47th president of the United States. The people of Danish Greenland woke up to find themselves being glowered at by the hungry monster of Trump's economic expansionism, Canada prepares to be mauled by high U.S. trade tariffs, while Panama, like Colombia, is steeling itself for combat with the beast it recently saw as a cooperative neighbour. It is clear that there will be tough times for almost everyone outside the Oval Office – at least for the next four years – and Ukraine's economic, political and moral woes look set to become even more complicated.

Ukrainians have continued to monitor the slow but steady advance of Russian troops in Donbas while actively discussing one of Trump's latest orders: a 90-day suspension of all U.S.A.I.D. grant programmes pending a full audit of funds already spent. At the same time, the U.S. has temporarily closed its doors to Ukrainian refugees.

On social networks, there was some sympathy for people trying to enter or remain in the U.S. as refugees, but the suspension of funding for U.S.A.I.D. programmes provoked almost wild enthusiasm in some sections of Ukrainian society.

Marian Zablotsky, a young but well-known Member of

Parliament from the Servant of the People party, wrote: "I wholeheartedly support the suspension of U.S.A.I.D. projects and their audit. There are currently 112 such projects active in Ukraine, accounting for $7 billion, the expenditure for which is scheduled annually. It seems like everything is fine (regarding these grants), but it is not. The first problem is that almost all of these projects are reduced to endless round tables and conferences and they are, therefore, talentless and meaningless, but the main problem is that most of this money remains in the United States as the net profit of the private companies which implement the grants."

Half of Zablotsky's followers agreed with her and launched a campaign on social networks featuring mock grief for U.S.A.I.D. grantees. The other half stood up for organisations affected by Trump's decision. The employees of these N.G.O.s must be in a stupor as they face the possibility that funding may not be resumed after the audit.

One of the organisations that has suffered from Trump's decision is Ukraïner Media, a powerful creative agency that, before the start of a full-scale war, created high-quality video and online content about Ukraine and its attractions for local and foreign audiences. After February 24, 2022, the agency became involved in war journalism, regularly reporting from the front lines, while continuing to publish books and implementing other patriotic projects.

"Yes, Ukraïner Media is between 80 and 90 per cent. dependent on U.S.A.I.D. and, in the absence of a way out of this crisis, most of our products will disappear within a few months," said the agency's founder, Bohdan Logvinenko. "Unfortunately, however, this does not mean that other media will occupy the niches that we and other organisations dependent on American funding used to occupy. Instead, very different media forces will step in and you will not even notice how everything around you suddenly becomes swamped with oligarchic or Russian content. For example, we will no longer be able to film our Units series of war reports, since they are very expensive to make. We could produce them more cheaply without visiting the front line, but quality will be sacrificed."

Logvinenko does not believe that U.S.A.I.D. funding will be resumed and is looking for donors and sponsors among ordinary Ukrainians and the Ukrainian business community. The heads of many other U.S.-funded non-governmental organisations and independent media groups have decided to follow the same path.

It is interesting that those who dislike the recipients of U.S. grants call them "Sorosites", meaning "the children" of George Soros. This term is more than twenty years old and was, at first, neutral, but during the fight against Soros' projects in Russia, an unjustly negative connotation was attached to it. In the end, Russia declared the "Sorosites" foreign agents and expelled them from their territory. At the same time, pro-Russian media outlets in Ukraine, such as Strana, began to lash out with criticism at everyone involved in projects financed by Soros' Open Society Foundation.

The Soros Foundation continues to operate in Ukraine, providing, for example, financial support for libraries damaged by Russian attacks, but the pejorative term "Sorosites" is still used by some commentators for any foreign-funded N.G.O.s and media projects.

A closer look at those who are rejoicing over the end of funding for U.S.A.I.D. projects reveals that many of them are former representatives of pro-Russian parties or individuals with pro-Russian views. These elements have started "performing" like an orchestra on social networks. Zablotsky's statement quoted above was almost immediately reposted 2,000 times. One can only guess at the location of the conductor of this ensemble.

In a recent interview with the Italian *Il Folio* newspaper, President Zelensky said that the war had made Ukrainians more aggressive. I have to agree. The verbal aggression directed at U.S.A.I.D. grantees is tame compared to the recent attacks against one of Ukraine's best-known journalists, Vitaly Portnikov. Someone – possibly on Russian orders – extracted a one-minute clip from a long video interview made a year ago, in which Portnikov explained why the children of Ukrainian M.P.s and officials were not fighting at the front. For the last two weeks social media and YouTube blogger chats have been at fever-pitch, pouring spleen over Portnikov and what he is supposed to have said.

Yes, there is more aggression in Ukrainian life and the two main reasons for this are related to Russia: one cause is the war itself, but informational and psychological operations organised by Russian Special Services are also having an effect. Ukrainians are frequently led astray by fake or provocative "news" created from old and edited video material and disseminated on Telegram channels.

President Trump's outrageous statements about using military force to take over Greenland and Panama and welcoming Canada as the 51st state have made it very difficult for Ukrainians to determine whether what they read on the Internet is fictional or true.

It would, of course, be more productive if Ukrainians stopped arguing about American government grants or what journalists like Vitaly Portnikov said or did not say and started to focus on Trump. However, anyone wishing to have a meaningful discussion about the new U.S. President requires a knowledge of anthropology, psychology, gerontology, political science and world history, as well as a limitless imagination. It is rare to find all this in one person and I too am unable to explain why Trump's attitude to the world community is so similar to Putin's. Can Putin's annexation of Crimea be compared with Trump's desire to take control of an island belonging to Denmark? Are all Trump's predatory statements designed to prove to Putin that the U.S. and Russian Presidents are psychologically and ideologically identical – twin brothers who should be able to find a common language? If Trump sees himself as evenly matched with Putin, has he decided that he needs to start grabbing mineral-rich territories before Russia does? Or is Trump, perhaps, anxious about a possible Russian nuclear attack on the U.S. from the North Pole?

In any case, heated conversations over Greenland are distracting people from the job of achieving peace in Ukraine. Trump himself, it seems, is distracted by his "Greenland idea" and other geopolitical fantasies, but we can be sure that Putin allows nothing to distract him, although I can imagine the warmth of feeling with which he is watching Donald Trump flaunt his territorial ambitions. Putin would probably like to seize Greenland himself and hold a referendum there in Russian style.

The appetites of the Russian Empire cannot be satisfied by a diet of independent states with universally recognised borders. Russia has not recognised borders for a long time, but there is one factor that limits Putin's appetite: all the Russian referendum organisers, all his "little green men", are busy fighting Ukraine or occupying parts of it. If a ceasefire is signed, Russian troops and special forces will find themselves less tied up. In which direction will Putin then turn his hungry gaze? He has many claims against countries with which Russia shares a border, but he is also interested in territories located thousands of kilometres away. Surely, he will want to capitalise on the many years he has spent meddling in the Middle East and Africa.

15.02.2025

On a Wing and a Prayer

Whenever the situation on the front lines worsens – straining Ukrainians' already taut nerves – articles appear in the media about the imminent resumption of air traffic: the reopening of Ukraine's airports and airlines that are on the verge of relaunching operations inside the country without waiting for the end of the war or the signing of a peace treaty. Trump's desire to turn every issue into a business deal, his willingness to talk to Putin and his apparent conviction that the Russian President wants peace have thrown Ukrainians into fits of panic and, right on cue, news reports have appeared declaring the readiness of foreign airlines to relaunch flights from Ukrainian airports.

As if to prove that this news is more than an attempt by the government to quell the tide of pessimism, on February 11, a delegation of top managers from Kyiv's main airport, Boryspil, went to Budapest for negotiations with the Hungarian airline Wizz Air. The talks lasted three days and ended just before the start of the Munich Security Conference, where, as in recent years, the main topic was the war in Ukraine.

Ukrainians paid little attention to the "aviation news". They are used to living without airports. We can make do, as a hundred years ago, with road and rail transport. President Zelensky and his delegation most likely started their journey to Munich on a train bound for Poland.

The Ukrainian Parliament, meanwhile, has made two decisions which are as unexpected as they are unpopular. The Parliament voted to purchase two old Russian nuclear reactors from Bulgaria for installation at the existing Khmelnitsky Nuclear Power Plant. The other surprise was a vote establishing February 24 as a National Day of Prayer.

Ukrainians understand the need to shore up the country's energy infrastructure, but they cannot be expected to welcome an old, Russian reactor as a good buy. Safety is seen as paramount and many Ukrainians consider the purchase a betrayal of national interests.

The establishment of February 24 as a National Day of Prayer brought a sad smile to our faces as we remembered the hyperbolic role of the Church in Russia and how Russian priests bless ballistic missiles directed at Ukrainian cities.

I must admit that the recent wave of panic and pessimism has hit me too. I stay afloat by remembering how, at the end of 2022, I was full of optimism about Ukraine's ability to liberate its captured territories and I felt this optimism in my friends and colleagues. At that time only around 10 per cent. of Ukrainians were ready to exchange territories for peace. Today, this number is perhaps as high as 50 per cent., but the other half of the population has become more entrenched – unable to envisage a lasting peace without the complete liberation of Ukraine from the Russian occupiers. There are no calls for peace in exchange for territories in the public media space. Those who would countenance such a deal keep quiet. They are afraid of being declared traitors, while the voices against peace in exchange for chunks of Ukraine can be heard every day, loud and clear.

They have nothing to fear. No-one will criticise you for patriotism.

Ukrainians have had plenty of cause to think about the sacrifices made in this war – about the victims of Bucha, Borodyanka, Mariupol, Bakhmut, the soldiers who have been killed, badly wounded or imprisoned, or who are still fighting, and about the sacrifices made by their families. If Ukraine is forced to give up its territories, if the U.S., E.U. and N.A.T.O. do not provide Ukraine with security guarantees, then what were all these sacrifices for?

In whatever direction the current drive towards negotiations goes, Ukraine's future relations with Russia will be determined by the memory of the injustice and cruelty of their aggression. Perhaps the first National Day of Prayer will be dedicated to the memory of the Ukrainians who have died in this war – both military and civilian. Such an event may unite a tired and partially hopeless nation.

Today, more than ever, Ukrainians need optimism – something to maintain their faith in a just end to the war. The U.S. will survive without Ukraine's rare earth metals, but without optimism and faith Ukraine will not.

17.02.2025

Love in the Time of Trump

The Munich Security Conference coincided with Valentine's Day, but the only reference to love was a negative one when Vance chose to pour cold water on the United States' relationship with Europe by listing Europe's "faults" as he sees them.

Words of love were much louder in Lviv, at the Lychakiv Cemetery, where Natalia Palamarchuk read poems at the graveside of her husband Vasyl, who died in combat last year. She went to the cemetery by herself, leaving her three children at home. On Valentine's Day she wanted to be alone with her husband of 21 years. Vasyl Palamarchuk is one of more than a hundred Ukrainian writers and poets killed in this war.

Ukrainians did not give much thought to Valentine's Day this year. After Trump's telephone conversation with Putin some Ukrainians were overcome with despair while others were furious. Social networks are still filled with pessimism and dire predictions. They see Ukraine lying on the operating table between two macabre surgeons, scalpels in hand.

Trump's 90-minute conversation with Putin instantly boosted the Russian economy. Share prices rose and the rouble increased in value against the dollar. Ukrainians understood that the call was not a conversation between the leader of the democratic world and an autocratic aggressor.

Rather, it was a discussion between two businessmen who were focused on trade relations, both keen to re-engage in mutually beneficial deals and clear away any obstacles to them, notably Ukraine and the war-induced sanctions against Russia.

Trump has, no doubt, greatly pleased Russian politicians with a post on X, calling President Zelensky a dictator. With this statement, he took the side of Putin, whom, apparently, he does not consider a dictator. The balance of world power has changed dramatically. It seems that, with Trump's help, Putin will try to achieve in Ukraine what the Russian army, supported by North Korean forces, has failed to do: subdue Ukraine.

The sixteen-year-old daughter of Natalia Vorozhbit, a well-known Ukrainian playwright, could not hold back tears after reading Trump's statements. "It is better to live under bombs than under the conditions of these two cynics' peace," she cried. "Under bombs there is hope that you may not be struck, but under this imposed peace there is no such hope."

While Zelensky was speaking in Munich about the need for unity in Ukrainian society, a number of well-known Ukrainian human rights N.G.O.s and activists were criticising him. Before leaving for Munich, President Zelensky had signed the decision of the National Security and Defence Council on the introduction of sanctions against a number of oligarchs. The list includes the country's fifth president, Petro Poroshenko, who could not go to Munich because every day before and during the conference he was summoned to answer investigators' questions and to defend himself from the National Security and Defence Council's accusations of treason. All of Poroshenko's assets have been frozen and his foundation, which has been purchasing weapons and ammunition for the Ukrainian army, can no longer function.

"Sanctions cannot serve as a tool in bringing to justice those who commit criminal offences," human rights organisations said in a joint statement. "Sanctions cannot replace criminal responsibility because the principles of justice are undermined by the political motives that guide the authors of the sanctions. The use of sanctions instead of an investigation and fair trial means the destruction of democracy in Ukraine."

Petro Poroshenko is still the leader of the opposition and the head of the European Solidarity parliamentary party. Perhaps this latest attack on him was prompted by the prospect of presidential elections on which the White House has been insisting.

Trump is also demanding guaranteed access to Ukrainian rare earth metals. Having decided to move relations with Ukraine, including military concerns, onto a commercial footing, Trump is leaving Ukraine little room for manoeuvre. President Zelensky had promised the Americans these metals in exchange for continued military aid, but the initial version of the agreement proposed by the U.S. Secretary of the Treasury did not mention any guarantees of aid or security for Ukraine and was rejected by Zelensky at the last moment.

A significant proportion of Ukraine's rare earth metal deposits is located in territories occupied by Russia, including Donbas and part of Zaporizhzhia region. These rare earth metals are of interest to both Russia and China, and private Chinese companies have set their sights on deposits in the occupied territories, apparently intending to build extraction and enrichment plants there. Perhaps Russia plans to use the metals to pay China for support in the war against Ukraine. Or perhaps, due to sanctions, Russia finds itself unable independently to develop the deposits and needs Chinese investment to exploit them effectively. To date Ukrainian intelligence agencies have identified more than ten private Chinese companies already working in occupied Ukrainian territory, doing preparatory work to restore destroyed infrastructure.

*

The third anniversary of the full-scale war with Russia and the eleventh anniversary of Russia's first military attack on Ukraine and the annexation of Crimea have attracted a new wave of foreign journalists who are more interested in the opinion of Ukrainians about the possibility of ending the war this year than in the situation at the front, which is approaching stalemate. Ukrainian troops have learned to use combat drones to prevent the movement of Russian ammunition and equipment deep behind enemy lines and the Russian army is advancing only very slowly and at a very high cost in lives. In some places, including near Pokrovsk, Ukrainian troops have halted the Russian offensive and even liberated several settlements.

The Ukrainian military does not believe in the possibility of signing a peace treaty with Putin. It is determined to continue fighting although it complains about exhaustion and the lack of a demobilisation system or even regular rotation.

Attacks against soldiers who are serving away from the front continue, although the Russian special services have changed their strategy. They used to recruit young and thoughtless saboteurs and arsonists on social networks, but recently they have taken to tricking unsuspecting Ukrainian citizens into becoming human bombs. A person is promised money for delivering a package and when they calmly arrive at the entrance of the mobilisation centre or some other place where soldiers or potential soldiers are gathered, the bomb inside the package is detonated via a telephone call from Russia or from the occupied territories or, sometimes, from a nearby location.

The other day, a woman and three military sappers were killed, and six others seriously wounded, when the shopping bag that the woman was delivering to an address in Mykolaiv exploded. Russian media proudly report such "successes" as evidence of an armed, Ukrainian, pro-Russian underground movement. The Russian people seem to need this "evidence" to feel that victory for their army is coming closer.

On February 14, in the middle of the Munich Security Conference, I was afraid that a terrorist attack would target the romantic train journeys organised by the Ukrainian railways specially for the families of military personnel. Ukrzaliznytsia ran the "St Valentine's Trains" out of Kyiv and Lviv. Soldiers could buy a compartment for themselves and their loved ones and spend two hours on a train that took them on a ride around the city. Thankfully, the St Valentine's Day train rides went off without a single act of sabotage.

February 14 is behind us, as is the Munich Security Conference. Ahead is an unpredictable future in which Europe can no longer count on U.S. support as Trump distances himself further and further from a Ukraine suspended between the fourth year of full-scale war and negotiations with Russia – negotiations in which Europe will not take part and the American "partners" are more interested in the speed at which an agreement can be reached than in protecting Ukrainian interests and achieving a just peace.

20.02.2025

Remembering

Almost three years ago, on February 24, 2022, several explosions were heard in Kyiv at five in the morning. Millions of Ukrainians were woken up by the war. No-one went to work. The stores did not open. Anyone who had plans for that day forgot about them. The day of the week no longer mattered. A different calendar came into force, one marked only by military action: the number of downed planes, destroyed tanks, killed or wounded soldiers, the distance in kilometres between you and the advancing Russian troops.

I also woke up that Thursday at five o'clock in the morning. Running to the window, I stood looking down at the empty street, at the small square opposite our apartment building, at my beloved city, where the first Russian missiles had just exploded. I stood there for about 40 minutes. Then two more missiles exploded somewhere to the south-east, and I finally understood that a war had begun, a big war that would change my life, the life of my family and the lives of tens of millions of people in Ukraine and far beyond its borders.

That day Russian missiles exploded in almost all regions of Ukraine, attempting to strike paralysing fear into the hearts of the population, to show the irrevocable force of Russia's intentions. As kilometre-long columns of their military hardware crossed from Belarus and Russia and headed towards Kyiv, troop carriers swooped down on the capital's military airfields in Hostomel and Vasilkov, and Russian Black Sea Fleet landing ships prepared to attack Odesa. A period of terrifying upheaval had begun which was supposed to lead to the disappearance of Ukraine from the map of the world. Vladimir Putin, in several speeches, declared this to be the aim of his "special military operation".

It feels much longer than three years. Indeed, Russia's aggression had started eight years earlier, in the winter and spring of 2014, with the annexation of Crimea and the beginning of the war in Donbas, but until February 2022 very few Ukrainians understood the horror and hardship that the people of those regions had suffered. Shame on us and the international community which hardly reacted to those events.

When the independence of the entire country was at stake, Ukrainians who had survived the economic chaos following the fall of the Soviet Union, the silent stand-off in the Orange Revolution and the murderous battles on the Maidan now faced death at the hands of a neighbour who was determined to take revenge on them for treasuring independence, for loving freedom, for their loud remembering of all the tsarist and Soviet crimes against Ukraine, its culture and its language.

Another event occurred on February 24, 2022, one that has influenced the course of this war but is rarely mentioned: President Zelensky, elected by 73 per cent. of voters, ceased to be an amateur, populist politician and became a responsible statesman. It is a pity that this did not happen in 2019, on his victory in the election, but at least it happened in 2022. His energy and self-confidence, his belief that Ukraine could defend itself, gradually seeped under the skin of the country's citizens.

21.02.2025

Still Playing Russian Roulette

Last night, on hearing a hum outside in the street, my wife Elizabeth got up and opened the window. The layer of snow covering the city had deadened all sound and she wanted to make sure it was an air raid alert and not some other noise. The open window, however, immediately allowed her to recognise the buzzing of drone engines passing directly above our apartment building.

Slamming the window shut and leaping away from the glass, Elizabeth waited for the explosions. They did not come. Only some minutes later several volleys of artillery fire sounded – the air defence team had waited until the drones had cleared the densely populated city centre.

I do not know if it was one of these drones that flew on and fell within the city limits of Bila Tserkva, 75 kilometres south-west of Kyiv. The explosion damaged houses and incinerated several cars. So far, there are no reports of casualties.

Last night, Ukraine's skies were visited by 160 Russian drones. Eighty-seven of them were shot down. The rest either hit their targets or fell on open ground, redirected there by electronic defence systems.

The war has long since turned into "Russian roulette" for Ukraine's civilian population. Residents of cities located closer to the front line or on the coast are in the greatest danger of falling victim to this cruel sport. Odesa has been without electricity or heating for several days due to drone attacks on infrastructure. It is −10°C in Kyiv and, although my apartment is warm, I want to go to our house in the country where it is easier to get a good night's sleep, away from the noise of sirens. True, if air defence crews target the Russian drones flying over our village on their way to Kyiv, everyone is woken by the shots and nobody sleeps until the morning.

At the very beginning of the full-scale war, in February 2022, my village neighbour, 78-year-old Tolik, promised not to shave his beard until the Ukrainian army defeated the Russians. I have several photographs of him from back then. You can see how his beard grew long due to the lack of victory. But recently I have noticed that Tolik's beard has become shorter. I asked him if he had lost hope of our overcoming the Russian aggression, but Tolik stubbornly repeated that he would not shave until Ukraine's victory was sealed. I could not understand what was going on until Tolik's wife, Nina, secretly admitted that she had grown fed up with her husband's unkempt appearance and had taken to trimming his beard at night, while he slept. Tolik looks as well-groomed as if he was making regular trips to the barber.

People in the village no longer talk about victory. The main topic of conversation is Trump and how America has betrayed Ukraine and sided with Putin. There is also talk about recent funerals. During the first two years of war no soldiers from the community died and the local folk were proud of this, as if there were some kind of magic power protecting their people from harm. Today, though, the village has dead and missing, presumed dead, soldiers and those who have returned home without limbs. It is no longer any different from neighbouring communities where grieving villagers have long dreamed of an end to the war, though they talk about it cautiously and without much optimism.

"I don't think the war will end any time soon," our old friend Svetlana told me. A year ago she returned to Kyiv after almost two years living as a refugee in Bulgaria. "You can't trust inadequate politicians," she continued. "And now, instead of one of them, we have two: Putin and Trump!"

I didn't want to argue with Svetlana, but I want to believe that the war will end this year and not the way Putin wants it to end. We have to wait and see, and we have to survive because Ukraine will need all of us after the war – to help the country heal and recover. After the war, we will all become doctors for Ukraine.

24.02.2025

Three Years on Fire

There is a Russian tradition that always evokes a sarcastic smile in Ukrainians: each year must be dedicated to some important topic around which Russian society should unite. So, 2015 was the "Year of Literature" – patriotic literature, of course; 2016 was the "Year of Cinema". President Putin declared 2017 the "Year of Memory and Glory in Russia". Hundreds of patriotic events were organised at public expense. But President Putin declared 2024 the "Year of the Family" – a year during which hundreds of thousands of Russian soldiers would die, turning wives into widows and leaving children fatherless.

There is no such tradition in Ukraine. If a year is named at all, it is according to the Chinese calendar. In 2025, the wooden snake has replaced the wooden dragon, but I think it is possible to give each year of the full-scale Russian–Ukrainian war its own name.

And 2022 was the "Year of Shocks and Cautious Optimism". After Russia's unsuccessful attack on Kyiv, the enemy retreated to Belarus and Ukrainian troops liberated captured territories in Kharkiv region. President Zelensky promised new counterattacks and Western partners promised significant military aid. All Ukrainians, both military and civilian, saw victory just around the corner.

But then came 2023, which I would call the "Year of

Dashed Hopes". Ukrainians were expecting a powerful counteroffensive and the liberation of the rest of the occupied territories. The Chief Military Intelligence Officer of Ukraine, General Budanov, promised that soon we would be drinking coffee on the seafront in Yalta, on the Crimean Peninsula. Alas, the counteroffensive did not take place. The lack of weapons and ammunition must have figured high on the list of reasons for this. I had the constant impression that our Western partners were delivering weapons with a calculated delay of several months and almost always in smaller quantities than promised. It became impossible to plan any military operations except defensive ones. A counteroffensive requires a huge stockpile of weapons, which could not be built up given the slow and unpredictable deliveries. Among ordinary Ukrainians, disappointment was accompanied by anger rather than depression.

I call 2024 the "Year of Getting Real". The word "victory", trumpeted in the Ukrainian media throughout 2022 and 2023, almost disappeared from use. Ukraine's unexpected attack on the Kursk region of Russia was a surprise that pleased some but angered others, who thought it would have been better to use the scarce resources to strengthen the defence of Donbas and the south of Ukraine. For more than six months, however, Ukrainian troops have held on in Kursk region, and this territory may play a positive role in any negotiations with Russia aimed at bringing a halt to the fighting. Optimists say that these territories could be exchanged for captured Ukrainian territories. Pessimists believe that the Kremlin regime does not care about this bit of Kursk region or its population. Russia has been bombing the area mercilessly, sparing no thought for the local population or infrastructure. The enemy is confident that Ukraine will not remain there forever, just as they believe that captured territories, including Crimea and Donbas, will never be returned to Ukraine. As long as Russia can sell oil and gas, Putin will have the financial resources to fund the army and pump money into subsidising these captured and badly damaged territories.

Like every Ukrainian, I would like to see a happy conclusion to this war in the near future. Surely a superhero, individual or collective, will suddenly act to turn things around. The Ukrainian army is undoubtedly a collective superhero, but one that is tired and lacks weapons and ammunition. The Ukrainian people are also a collective superhero, but cracks in their unity are beginning to show. They are exhausted and traumatised by three years of constant stress and the emotional rollercoaster that is wartime life.

Whenever I read the results of sociological surveys in Ukraine about ordinary Ukrainians' hopes of victory, I wonder in which of the four "Ukraines" this survey was conducted. I know the answer, of course. Polls are always conducted on the territory controlled by the Ukrainian government which is more than 70 per cent. of the territory of the Ukrainian state, but the responses must be primarily those of Ukrainians who are still able to live at home – people who are more comfortable and feel more confident than refugees, temporarily displaced persons and Ukrainians who remained in the occupied territories. We do not know the thoughts of Ukrainians who are living under occupation.

Nor do we know the opinion of Ukrainians who became refugees abroad – more than seven million, including more than half a million children. The longer the war lasts, the less likely it is that they will return to Ukraine. Those who do not believe that peace and stability will be restored in the foreseeable future have already decided not to return.

Let us consider the occupied territory as one "Ukraine", Ukrainian refugees abroad as another, then Ukrainians living in their own homes as a third and Ukrainian Internally Displaced Persons as a fourth "Ukraine". This last category amounts to about six million people. Most of their homes have been destroyed. I doubt we will find many optimists among them. At the end of 2024, however, Ukrainian sociological services reported that 83 per cent. of Ukrainians still believe in victory. Perhaps the word "victory" has changed its meaning here, or do they believe in the appearance of a superhero who will miraculously save Ukraine from the monster that is Russia?

I am not a careless optimist. I am a pragmatic optimist, and, oddly enough, my current optimism is connected with President Trump, who from the very beginning of his presidential term began to imitate Putin's geopolitical recklessness. Putin annexed Crimea and seized Donbas and part of southern Ukraine. Trump has made outlandish statements about wanting Greenland, Canada and Panama to belong to the United States. A new Trump seems to be emerging – an even more unpredictable force which shows no respect for international law or territorial sovereignty and uses the terminology of cut-throat big business to announce policy and make his threats.

At the same time, Trump's favourite slogan, "Make America Great Again", gives some grounds for optimism. It seems impossible to make America great again while Putin is trying to make Russia great again. The U.S. and Russia cannot be great at the same time, and the U.S. has more resources than Putin's Russia.

If Ukraine is forced to give up territory, this will be seen as evidence that no country was powerful enough to keep Russia from overthrowing a world order based on respect for sovereignty and state borders. Yes, I understand that even if a ceasefire is declared and negotiations begin, they could drag on endlessly because Russia will not agree to withdraw from the captured territories and Ukraine will never give them up. Trump will put pressure on both Putin and the Ukrainian President, and the process will continue – a process resembling a wrestling match between two ageing machos watched by Ukraine, Europe and the rest of the world.

28.02.2025

The White House Reality Show

It is warming up in Kyiv. The temperature has risen from −5°C to 4°C. Sometimes, the sun peeps through breaks in the clouds, but this has not brought much cheer to the citizens. They have not been watching for signs of spring as they usually do at this time of year. The atmosphere in the city and in the country as a whole has been one of nervous expectation, though with no hope of an end to military action or the signing of a peace treaty with Russia – nothing so specific. Indeed, it was not clear what we were waiting for, but it was something connected with Donald Trump and the change in U.S. policy towards Ukraine.

Clarity emerged during today's macabre piece of White House theatre: handshakes, a thumbs up and some fist pumps from the U.S. President before he sat down with Volodymyr Zelensky to discuss a minerals-for-war-support deal and to humiliate him. As air raid warnings sounded in northern and eastern Ukraine, Trump and his associates proved that their interests are more closely aligned with those of Putin than with those of the Ukrainian people, the rule of law or the independence of sovereign states. Very soon all talks were off the table and Zelensky was gone.

What occurred in front of the television cameras was chilling and extraordinary. Zelensky grave, angry, desperate – as befits a leader being obliged to bargain away his nation's birthright. Trump claiming to be the honest broker, saying: "I am not aligned with anybody. I am aligned with the world." Be thankful, he tells a man who has seen his people murdered, his territory captured and besieged. "Make a deal or we're out."

It got worse. Zelensky showed him photographs of war atrocities. "I think President Trump is on our side," he said, with no genuine hope and certainly no expectation that that was true. Vice President J.D. Vance attacked Zelensky for being disrespectful. Both Trump and Vance verbally pummelled him for the cameras, for this is the art of the deal now: loaded, hectoring, callous, bloodless.

Ukrainians' belief in a concrete proposal from Trump to end the war was replaced by the conviction that the President has no such plan, but rather a plethora of half-baked ideas about U.S. involvement in the region – ideas that often relate to Ukraine, but sometimes conflict with each other and are never focused on supporting a country that is the victim of Russian aggression.

During the past two weeks, we have watched as the issue of ending the Russian–Ukrainian war has transformed into the issue of rare earth metal mining in our country. During the Russian–U.S. negotiations in Saudi Arabia the participants also discussed the extraction of rare earth metals, only they focused on resources in Russian territories and in the occupied territories of Ukraine. These rare earth metals have pushed the topic of the war and military aid to Ukraine out of the media space. That space has been filled with dollars.

Older Ukrainians, who grew up in the Soviet Union, recognise in this situation the United States that was depicted by Soviet propaganda cartoons: a nation of greedy, irresponsible, grab-what-you-can capitalists, who spat on complex problems and had eyes only for dollar superprofits.

This is an existential war, and a new reality. Trump says Zelensky is "not ready for peace", but Ukraine has no choice but to fight on, whatever the cost. Aid that was previously given for nothing must now be bought. If there is no money, then it is necessary to pay with resources. After three years of full-scale Russian aggression, U.S. geopolitical interests in Ukraine have been replaced by financial interests. Instead of the politician President Biden, the businessman President Trump has entered the arena.

Note that the U.S. proposal on the extraction of rare earth metals in Ukraine, if realised, would allow the U.S. to sign a similar agreement with Russia and start digging without waiting for the end of hostilities. The notion is an "investment fund", managed by the United States and Ukraine on "equal terms", into which Ukraine would contribute 50 per cent. of future proceeds from state-owned mineral resources, oil and gas "to promote the safety, security and prosperity of Ukraine". Trump insists it is "very fair".

Would such an agreement encourage Russia to cease its aggression? No! Does it contain security guarantees for Ukraine? It seems not. Does Ukraine have any choice? Debatable.

In this situation, Britain and the E.U. become much more important partners for Ukraine than before. While organising favourable access to Ukrainian resources for the U.S., Trump hopes to hand over to Europe and Britain responsibility for Ukraine's security in the event of a cessation of hostilities, and responsibility for further military assistance. Given this, it is by no means clear what advantage any agreement on rare earth metals would give Ukraine.

Trump's claims that U.S. mining on Ukrainian territory will be a sufficient guarantee of Ukraine's security because Russia will not risk attacking U.S. economic interests do not stand up to criticism. The Chinese state-owned C.O.F.C.O. corporation invested in a new grain and oil handling complex in Ukraine's Mykolaiv port, but Chinese involvement did not protect the port from being targeted by Russian missiles. It has not been operational since March 2022 and the region is losing about 40 per cent. of its revenues.

The fact that Trump has been so complimentary about Vladimir Putin, and so hostile to Zelensky, says everything. "I think he will keep his word," Trump assured the world. "I have known him for a long time." Trump's phrase that peace will be achieved "fairly soon or it won't happen at all" indicates that he will not waste too much time on negotiations with Putin if they drag on, or if Putin puts forward conditions that are unacceptable to Ukraine. Some conditions have been announced by Sergei Lavrov, the Russian Foreign Minister, who reminded us that Russia still plans to seize the entirety of Kherson and Zaporizhzhia regions.

Zelensky was brave, but we are supplicants now. Trump and the Kremlin have made it abundantly clear that Ukraine's participation in the negotiations between the U.S. and Russia is not necessary or desirable. Like so much else, the principle announced by Biden ("Nothing about Ukraine without Ukraine") has been trampled underfoot. Zelensky was called to the White House to sign, but not speak.

Trump has had his way. He has transformed Ukraine from a subject into an object, and after this White House humiliation some Ukrainians are convinced that the extraction of rare earth metals on Trump's terms would turn our country into a "colony" of the United States. Still, many Ukrainians would prefer to live in a U.S. colony than in a Russian one, if that is the choice.

13.03.2025

War and Europe

Each war in Europe has changed the borders of states and continued to affect the lives of citizens long after the cessation of the armed struggle. Each war has ended with the restoration of destroyed cities, trampled principles and a new recipe for lasting peace. After each war, the phrase "Never again!" has hung in the air.

In the end, to protect itself from war, and ensure badly needed economic growth, Europe decided to become smaller and more united. This is how the European Union came into being. Thanks to this new configuration, the events of 1992 in Transnistria (Moldova) did not affect Europe, and the military action in the former Yugoslavia did not become a European war. Thanks to this, the annexation of Crimea and the occupation of part of Donbas in 2014 did not impede trade between the European Union and Russia. Those acts of violence were dismissed as local issues in faraway lands. Europe's stated democratic values could be demonstrated by symbolic, localised sanctions that did not prevent members of the E.U. from continuing to enjoy "fruitful" trade with the Russian Federation.

It seems that no-one in Europe expected the events in Crimea and Donbas to become a prelude to a major military conflict, a war that Brussels and Berlin could not ignore, but that is what happened. The symbolic sanctions, designed to conceal sleepy Europe's *laissez-faire* attitude, were discredited as an instrument of pressure.

While the Belarusian dictator was blackmailing Poland and Lithuania with refugees specially "imported" into Belarus from South Asia, Russia was preparing a military operation compared to which Lukashenko's provocations would look like child's play. Today, three years after the start of Russia's full-scale aggression against Ukraine, Europe is looking at itself in the mirror and beginning to understand how much it has changed, how the lives of Europeans have changed, and what giant steps must be taken to save from destruction at least something of the old, familiar Europe – a community only just coming to the realisation that the fortress known as the European Union no longer ensures a problem-free and peaceful existence.

Some may say that the E.U. slept through the moment when it needed to wake up, gather strength, come to terms with the changed geopolitical situation in the world and deal with the threats to the values which it was assumed so robustly underpinned its existence.

The era of technocrat prime ministers and presidents lent sleeping Europe a blanket of "peace and prosperity" under which entire populations were happy to doze indefinitely. Europe remained in this state of cosy slumber for a long time, dreaming of the economic and political stability that had been a European reality for only a short period, since the Second World War, and in the lullaby that accompanied its sleep, the word "prosperity" was endlessly repeated. Peace was taken for granted.

And then the Russian aggression of 2022 woke people

up – not immediately, and not everyone, of course. Europe slept so deeply that even the slaughter of civilians in Mariupol and Bucha could not, it would seem, wake everyone. Today we can say that much of Europe is, at last, awake and blinking at the unfamiliar terrain that surrounds it – full of problems that demand urgent solutions.

What should the E.U. do, besides arm itself? Should it decrease in size and exclude unreliable Hungary and Slovakia, or expand to include Moldova and crippled Ukraine?

The Russian aggression achieved in three years what Ukrainian politicians failed to achieve during Ukraine's 34 years of independence: it turned the hearts of all Ukrainians towards Europe and caused the E.U. to move Ukraine to the category of "our countries" and cross it off its list of "other countries". At the same time, Ukrainian refugees have become "ours" and are perceived not as fleeing strangers, but as Europeans, while Ukrainian culture has been embraced as part of European culture. In spite of protests from Polish and Slovak farmers, Ukrainian agriculture has forged closer ties with European agriculture.

As a result of these shifts, the Russian–Ukrainian war is now more often perceived in Europe as a European–Russian war. Perhaps this is why the U.S. has suddenly turned its back on Europe and started questioning its own membership of N.A.T.O. Trump's election has meant that in the U.S. prosperity comes first and geopolitical reality comes second.

19.03.2025

Non-Essential Goods

"Trump has caused the collapse of the Ukrainian book market!" my Ukrainian publisher, Oleksandr Krasovytskyy, said sadly as soon as we sat down in Kyiv's Bar 13.

I knew that President Trump and Elon Musk had caused the sales of Tesla cars to plummet, but what did Ukrainian books have to do with U.S. policies?

"After the scandal in the Oval Office and the public humiliation of Zelensky by Trump and Vance, Ukrainians stopped buying books," Olexandr explained. "And not only books, but many other things that you can live without. Books were mostly purchased by active citizens. The scandal in Washington has left them depressed, and depressed people don't buy non-essentials."

"You know, alcohol sales in Ukraine have increased since Trump took office," said Alexey Volkov, an expert in the alcohol market and a sincere lover of good beer. This development is good for the market, but not necessarily good for Ukrainian society.

Trade in non-essential goods can easily be affected by the news. Bad news can turn alcohol into a "staple product", but there is only one quick and safe cure for it and that is good news, and you can't get that at the pharmacy.

Trump's ever-increasing capriciousness has led to ever-decreasing stability the world over and in Ukraine, where the unpredictable consequences of the U.S. President's attempts to end the war with Russia have resulted in such unprecedented levels of insecurity that a major shift in the status quo – perhaps even a national catastrophe – is expected at any moment. Indeed, as soon as Trump announced the end of U.S. military aid to Ukraine and a pause in intelligence sharing, Russian troops launched an offensive in Kursk region and drove the Ukrainian army out of the town of Sudzha and the villages surrounding it.

Russia has regained control of most of its territory captured by Ukrainian troops last summer. Some say that the Ukrainian troops left Kursk region voluntarily due to pressure from Trump, and that the withdrawal was necessary to facilitate the start of ceasefire negotiations with Russia. However, Ukrainian General Staff maps from March 16 show that fighting between Ukrainian and Russian troops continues on Russian territory, indicating that no order to withdraw has been given. We do, nevertheless, see the Russian army advancing and the Ukrainian army retreating.

There is bad news from Sumy region, along the northeastern border with Russia. Evacuation of civilians has intensified as Russia drops heavy bombs on the area, turning farms, homes and administrative buildings into ruins. The Ukrainian military reports that the enemy is accumulating manpower and equipment across the border, suggesting that Russia may soon try to open a new front by invading Ukraine from the north.

This news is at odds with Trump's stated intention to achieve a reliable truce in the coming days. On the other hand, negotiations between American politicians and the

Ukrainian delegation in Jeddah ended positively. As was stated in Saudi Arabia, Russia must show its desire to end the war and agree to a 30-day cessation of hostilities and the possible extension of the truce before peace talks between the two sides can begin.

Russia is in no hurry to respond positively to Trump's peace initiative, and this cannot but irritate the U.S. President. Trump's leadership style demands urgent results and soon his American voters, remembering the promise to "end the war in 24 hours", will start looking at the calendar. Trump has been in power for two months, but the Russian–Ukrainian war continues.

Russia's war against Ukraine is a hugely forceful process that has been gathering energy for eleven years. Russia has invested hundreds of billions of dollars in its efforts to take over Ukraine, sacrificing its economy and its relations with the West, and possibly risking its own future to wage a war that has become the Russian Federation's *raison d'être*, the climax of Tsar-President Putin's reign. How could the Russians agree to the demand of their eternal ideological enemy, the United States, that they stop shooting and sit down at the negotiating table? In principle this is possible, because in Russian political culture all key decisions are made by one person. In such a scenario, the U.S. and Europe would not stop being Russia's enemies and Russia would continue its war against Ukraine using the more covert methods which its special services have been honing for generations.

The activity of Russian special services on Ukrainian territory is growing more noticeable by the day. Ukrainian citizens, in search of easy money, become perpetrators of terrorist acts against the Ukrainian military and the civilian population. The arrest of Ukrainians who help the enemy to select missile and drone targets has become commonplace. This brings us back to the mental pressures experienced by conscientious Ukrainians today. The almost daily reports about traitors give no cause for optimism, although the detentions do indicate that our special services are hard at work in the territories controlled by the Ukrainian government. This was not always the case. Eleven years ago, the Ukrainian police and special services sometimes carried out the commands of pro-Russian forces and did not always protect the sovereignty of Ukraine as they do today.

We have been reminded of this by the recent decision of the European Court of Human Rights concerning events that occurred during the so-called "Russian Spring" in Odesa on May 2, 2014. The court in Strasbourg has finally identified those responsible, finding the Ukrainian state guilty of violating human rights, failing to prevent violence, and not taking timely action to rescue the pro-Russian activists who were inside the Trade Union House during a fire that killed more than 50 of them.

The court also found that Russia actively contributed to the destabilisation of the political situation in Odesa and other Ukrainian cities. The court's conclusions do not specifically mention the Odesa city authorities or the city police department whose actions contributed to the tragedy. During the street battles, the police stood by and allowed pro-Russian activists hiding behind them to shoot at pro-Ukrainian activists.

The deaths of several dozen of the pro-Russian activists

in the Trade Union House fire prevented Russia from achieving the goals of its Russian Spring operation and ended its attempt to seize power in Odesa with the help of civil unrest.

The day after the announcement of the European Court of Human Rights' decision, a high-profile murder occurred in Odesa. The victim was Demyan Ganul, a well-known right-wing radical activist, former head of the Odesa branch of the "Right Sector", and a participant in many political actions, including the events of May 2, 2014.

An anonymous offer of $10,000 for Ganul's murder recently appeared online and Ganul asked the security services for protection. On March 14, however, a former Ukrainian officer who had deserted from the army approached Ganul on the street, shot him three times, and calmly walked away. The killer was soon arrested, but this murder has shocked Ukrainians and reminded them that mortal danger can strike far away from the front and without an air raid warning.

Another incident that has further dented our confidence in Ukraine's social cohesion involved two teenage friends from Ivano-Frankivsk, one of our most patriotic cities. On the instructions of Russian controllers, the friends – fifteen and seventeen years old – rented an apartment near the train station in their hometown, and there assembled two bombs from components taken from a cache disclosed to them by their controller. One of the bombs exploded as they were carrying it to the train station, killing the older boy instantly and ripping off the legs of the fifteen-year-old. The second bomb, left in the apartment, exploded at the same time, causing a huge fire in the high-rise building. Both bombs were detonated remotely by a telephone call.

Perhaps these young people did not consider themselves traitors when they agreed the deal. They were promised $1,700. They were probably not among those who fell into depression because of the scandal in the Oval Office and it is unlikely that they were following the bad news from Kursk or Sumy. They simply lived in a big city and felt the need for some extra cash, though what they lacked most was a social conscience – an essential quality for a healthy society.

29.03.25

Thinking about the Future

"It doesn't surprise me that they're abolishing the Ministry of Education," my old friend Dima told me. "Judging by what Steve Witkoff said on the Fox channel, neither history nor geography are taught in America."

Team Trump's energetic but purposefully misdirected attempts to push the negotiation processes forward have left Ukrainians in shock. Each day reveals new depths in the Oval Office's inadequacy and we can only shrug when we hear things like "Putin is not a bad guy" or "I feel that he wants peace". President Volodymyr Zelensky said something similar after his election in 2019, when he promised to negotiate a peace deal with Vladimir Putin within twelve months or resign. Neither peace nor his resignation materialised. A full-scale war began and after three years of fierce fighting, it is no longer Zelensky but Witkoff who sees peace in Putin's eyes. Putin's eyes are very small and you would have to look very close to see anything in them, but Ukrainians have long stopped trying to fathom the Russian dictator.

With each day of the "peace talks", the Kremlin shells Ukrainian cities more and more intensively, using new tactics involving large and heavy "Geranium" drones which fly at an altitude of about 2,000 metres. It is almost impossible to shoot them down when they are that high in the sky. As a result, we have seen a sharp increase in the number of victims and extent of destruction caused by each attack. Another "new thing" is how, during a raid, a large number of drones head for one target. Recently, more than a dozen drones made a night attack on Khmelnitsky; then it was Odesa's turn, and a few nights ago Kyiv was targeted. My family, like many Kyivites, spent that night in the hallway, listening to drone explosions and air defence cannonades.

Marco Cervetti, a chef and the best-known promoter of Italian cuisine in Ukraine, does not sleep in the hallway. It's too uncomfortable. The hallway in his rented apartment is small, and Marco is big – six and a half feet tall. So he goes down to the bomb shelter in the basement of his building. This means he has got to know all his neighbours very well. Sometimes he takes a bottle of Sangiovese down there to share. Marco loves to socialise and cook pasta for his friends, but he can't invite anyone to his home. Long before February 2022, he rented an apartment in an old building next to the Office of the President, in the very centre of the government quarter. Only those who live or work there can get access. The military does not let anyone else past the checkpoints. So Marco often cooks dinner for friends at someone else's home or in a bar. I missed the last meal he prepared for friends at the Torf bar, ten minutes from my home, but we have already agreed that in April he will cook dinner at my place.

It's strange, but recently I have started thinking about the future and have already begun planning trips for the summer and autumn. This does not mean that I believe in a quick end to the war. For everyone in Ukraine, the war is a game of Russian roulette. You don't know when a rocket or a drone will explode near you. Every night and every day, rockets and drones kill and maim people, destroy homes and burn cars with passengers inside. You keep busy and you don't have time to dwell on it. You carry on, living cautiously, listening carefully, aware of every sound.

Occasionally you notice that you are worrying about some strange, quite insignificant problem. For example, I regularly find myself thinking about the taste of Artemovsk salt from Donbas. All my life I have bought and used this coarse-grained, whitish salt with bits of grit in it. When Russia occupied the town where the mine is situated, stocks were still available throughout Ukraine. But eventually stocks ran out and since then, instead of Artemovsk salt, we have had to make do with Turkish and Polish imports that have their own specific taste – very different from the salt I have enjoyed all my long life. To distract myself from this strange nostalgia I have almost stopped using salt altogether. Sometimes I use soy sauce instead.

The other day I learned that in Transcarpathia there is a ready-to-operate salt mine that could supply salt to all of Ukraine, but it is not working because the co-owners have quarrelled and cannot agree on some aspects of their joint business. A conflict in the salt business during a full-scale war seems absurd. But this is our reality. I only hope the salt-mine owners can reach an agreement soon so that production can start. I am very curious – will it taste like salt from Donbas? If so, I will have one less thing to worry about in my life.

04.04.2025

What Is in the Pipeline?

Kyiv mornings are very foggy. Car headlights can be barely visible at a distance of ten metres. Nature itself is making it hard to think about the future. You simply cannot imagine it. Reading the news does not help. I remember a time when a glance at the headlines told you where the world was heading, but today's news refutes yesterday's and is likely to be refuted itself tomorrow. The announcement of an "energy truce" – a partial ceasefire agreement under which Russia and Ukraine would not bomb each other's energy infrastructure – was followed by reports of renewed attacks on Ukrainian facilities. Headlines about the agreement between the U.S. and Ukraine on the joint exploitation of rare earth metal deposits were supplanted by articles explaining that the U.S. had added clauses to the treaty that were unacceptable to Ukraine and that the U.S. and Russia had begun negotiations on the joint extraction of rare earth metals in Russia. Analytical pieces about the impossibility of holding presidential and parliamentary elections in wartime Ukraine have been pushed aside by headlines indicating that the elections could take place this summer and that Zelensky has already begun instructing his entourage about preparations for them.

The media world seems as unstable as the weather. Sometimes it's sunny and warm, sometimes it's foggy and wet, and sometimes morning frosts cover the fresh spring grass. We probably need to wait out this between-seasons period and hope that more stable meteorological conditions will follow, but we cannot ignore media reports of government initiatives, which indicate either a sudden surge in the efficiency of individual ministries or the approach of elections.

If an election campaign is announced in the near future, the Ukrainian leadership will not be able to extend the period of martial law and then, *de jure*, the war will be at an end, even if Russian drones and missiles continue to explode in Ukrainian cities. The country will have to pretend that military action has ceased, and cancel the restrictions on freedom imposed under martial law. The most important of these restrictions is the ban on men of draft age travelling abroad. If this ban is lifted, many men will leave the country. Many will go to their wives and children sheltering in Europe and elsewhere. Others will simply want to breathe the air of freedom. Some will leave Ukraine forever, exhausted by their fear of being mobilised, their mistrust of the Ukrainian government and the stress of daily life and uncertainty. If you live next to Russia you can forget about stability, and that goes for Lithuania and Finland and Georgia as well as for Ukraine.

The Ministry of Social Policy clearly understands the danger of a mass exodus of men from Ukraine. "We must make Ukraine a better place to live. This is what the government is working on today," the Deputy Minister of Social Policy, Darina Marchak, said this week. She promises to expand the social housing programme, create attractive jobs with good salaries and improve densely populated urban areas, creating new bicycle paths, parks, attractive embankments, and so on. When dozens of smaller cities have been destroyed and the industrial zones of larger ones have been flattened by Russian missiles and drones, statements like this sound utopian to say the least. It feels like a plan for the distant future – a post-war and post-election future when the Ministry of Social Policy will be working hard to make the lives of Ukrainians as comfortable as possible. In short, these statements can be interpreted as part of the current government's election campaign and we can expect similar declarations from other ministries and departments.

The Kyiv School of Public Administration, an N.G.O., recently launched a campaign to recruit students for a free online course called "Veteran's Spouse", which is designed for the partners of soldiers who have returned from the war as well as for the partners of active military personnel, soldiers missing in action, and the widows and widowers of fallen soldiers. The course has a broad scope and highlights the provision of support for the whole family. The syllabus includes an introduction to psychological support for veterans and their families, lectures by experienced lawyers on the state policies which underpin support for veterans, and information about state medical programmes and programmes aimed at getting veterans back into civilian work.

Although all this is organised by a non-governmental educational institution, the course materials emphasise the government's responsibility for providing support for veterans and their families. The list of lecture topics even contains an axiom about trust in the government and authorities, and this lends the initiative, which is clearly useful to Ukrainian society, the flavour of an election campaign gambit.

Has this reactivation of political life distracted Ukrainians from what is happening at the front? Not yet. The vague expectation of elections remains free from thoughts of a political power struggle. This is interesting. Opposition leaders have not declared their readiness to stand as presidential candidates. Volodymyr Zelensky's only realistic competitor is the Ambassador of Ukraine to Great Britain, Valeriy Zaluzhny, a military general who continues to repeat that elections should be held only after war is at an end.

Just as they were gingerly eyeing the prospect of elections, Ukrainian citizens were thrown into confusion by military experts, who predict a large-scale Russia offensive that will last six to nine months and could allow the Russian army to advance along the 1,000-kilometre-long front. One of the sections of the front where military action is expected to intensify is Sumy region in northern Ukraine, on the border with Kursk region – an area already suffering from frequent and deadly missile attacks.

The Central Electoral Commission, meanwhile, has announced that Ukrainian refugees abroad will vote not by mail or electronic means, but at polling stations set up in areas with the largest concentration of Ukrainian citizens.

How and where the evacuated residents of Sumy region will be able to vote is not yet known. Moreover, according to the Central Electoral Commission, 56,000 voters who before the war lived in the now destroyed city of Bakhmut in Donbas still live at their pre-war addresses.

Yes, Putin regularly repeats that negotiations with

Zelensky are pointless because the President of Ukraine is not legitimate. Even President Trump is tired of these statements. Zelensky still has very high support at home – about 60 per cent. – and the chances of victory for any other presidential candidate are minimal. Putin no doubt understands this, but perhaps he is hoping that presidential and parliamentary elections will plunge Ukraine into political chaos and further destabilise society – a situation which Russian special services would be ready to exploit to the full.

The speculation about elections raises many questions to which we have no answers, at least for now. Were elections to happen, they could turn out to be a positive historical precedent or grounds for endless legal proceedings and further accusations of illegitimacy.

In Russia, political statements by Zelensky and other Ukrainian politicians are followed with interest and usually provoke ironic commentary. At the same time, Russian propaganda is working hard to create new myths about the invincibility of its army and heroic Russian soldiers. An iron pipe has unexpectedly become a new symbol of their courage. We are talking about the pipe via which Russian soldiers were able to enter territory in Kursk region held by the Ukrainian army. A year ago, the Russians carried out a similar operation during the battle for the city of Avdiivka in Donbas, during which about 150 Russian soldiers crawled two kilometres through an underground cast-iron pipe with a diameter of about one metre. This manoeuvre enabled them to capture a district of the city.

In the episode of pipeline "heroism" which took place in March during the battles for the Russian town of Sudzha, about 800 Russian soldiers were sent behind the Ukrainian army through a fifteen-kilometre pipe. Many soldiers suffocated on the way, but enough of them reached the other end and entered into battle with the Ukrainian army. The Russian command has awarded medals to 112 participants in this operation, which was named "Stream". Why the remaining 700 participants were not awarded medals is unknown, as is the number of soldiers who died inside the pipeline. Perhaps it was 112.

On March 25, in Yekaterinburg, in the grounds of the Orthodox Church of the Saviour on Spilled Blood, a sixteen-metre "model" of this pipe was installed as a monument to the courage of the Russian military. Churchgoers are offered the opportunity to crawl through this pipe so that they can feel like a Russian soldier.

Russian schoolchildren will undoubtedly read about "The Feat of the Pipe" in future editions of their history textbooks. Those books will be one of the reasons why Russia will remain a threat to Ukraine even after this war. At the moment, however, the danger posed by children who are being brought up to hate their western neighbour is not what worries Ukrainians most. They are more concerned about when and how military action will end.

So Much Left Unwritten – Epilogue

"My worst fears are coming true – I am part of a new Executed Renaissance," wrote Victoria Amelina in the preface to the book by the murdered Ukrainian poet Volodymyr Vakulenko. The book would not have appeared without Amelina. She was determined that Vakulenko's voice should not be silenced.

After men in Russian military uniform took the poet from his home in early March 2022, Victoria spent several months trying to discover his fate. Eventually, his body was found in an unmarked grave in the forest near the town of Izyum. By that time Amelina had dug up Vakulenko's handwritten diary which he had buried under a cherry tree in his parents' garden. She deciphered the text and prepared it for publication. This diary formed the basis of a book and from it we learn about Vakulenko's thoughts and feelings – what he worried about – while he and his son, who has special needs, lived under occupation. This was the last thing Vakulenko wrote, his final work.

Victoria Amelina's book *A Diary of War and Justice: Looking at Women who Look at War* was recently published simultaneously in the U.K. and France. This was Victoria's last work. She did not even have time to finish it. She was writing it while searching for Volodymyr Vakulenko's body.

She was still writing it when she was mortally wounded by a Russian missile in Kramatorsk.

If not for the war – the Russian aggression – Vakulenko and Amelina could have written many more books.

There is nothing more tragic than marking the anniversary of an ongoing war. An anniversary should be an occasion to sum up and reflect on results, but what are the results of this war? They can be calculated in the hundreds of thousands of lost lives, in the endless destruction of people's homes, gardens, vineyards, villages, cities, and the ruination of our forests, fields, factories and power plants. The results of the war can also be calculated in the number of destroyed libraries, theatres, universities, schools, printing houses, film studios and museums.

During a war the aggressor seeks to totally undermine the victims' right to culture, to shelter, to life. Sometimes it seems that culture has become the aggressor's main target – the victim they most wish to harm because a nation's culture sets it apart from other nations and simultaneously provides it with the motivation and strength to resist subjugation. It is precisely this function of culture – the preservation of identity – that has made Ukrainian culture a major target of aggression, and not for the first time.

As the war rages on, in universities and schools Ukrainian youth study the tragic history of the writers and poets of the first "Executed Renaissance": 250 young and active Ukrainian poets and writers who were detained by the Soviet authorities and then shot between 1937 and 1938. The works that these murdered writers did not manage to write and publish remain in our minds as a kind of phantom of Ukrainian literature – cultural riches that we can only imagine.

In the same way, we can imagine the phantom of Ukrainian architecture – hundreds of buildings that were never built because their potential creators were repressed. The phantom of Ukrainian fine art also looms over us in the thousands of murdered artists' unrealised canvases.

This phantom element of Ukrainian culture grows larger with each day of the Russian aggression. Unrealised Ukrainian culture is beginning to outweigh created works as the list of cultural figures killed by Russian weapons grows longer – a list which bears the names of more than a thousand writers, musicians, artists, film directors and actors.

More than a thousand Ukrainian cultural sites have been destroyed by the Russian army, but if there was a building, a painting or a monument, we may still have at least a photograph and the memory of what once existed.

The destruction of Ukrainian cultural monuments has felt like an axe chopping away at my roots. I remember when a Russian missile hit the house-museum of Ukraine's best-known naive artist, Maria Primachenko. I remember when another missile destroyed the museum of my favourite Ukrainian philosopher and poet, Grigory Skovoroda, who was born near Kharkiv in 1722. I recall the ruins of the Mariupol theatre with people sheltering inside it – all destroyed by a huge bomb dropped from an airplane. Then there was Odesa Cathedral, its roof split open to the sun's rays by yet another missile.

It has gradually become obvious that the bombs and missiles are not destroying historical buildings and their contents; they are trying to annihilate an entire culture. It has become clear that after the war, as well as the reconstruction of villages and towns, the restoration of culture will be required. Ukrainian literature, music and cinema – they have all been bled dry by this war. It pains me to write about this or even to think about it. This pain will remain. It will appear in the fabric of post-war Ukrainian culture.

Authors who survive will have to write books on behalf of their fallen colleagues as well as for themselves. We will all have to work much harder to fill, at least partially, the jagged empty spaces gouged into Ukrainian culture by Russia's bombs and missiles over the last three years.

02.09.2025

Afterword
The "Ukraine Factor"

It is becoming more and more difficult to predict the future. I don't even try to imagine what might happen tomorrow morning. Nothing in the current geopolitical state of affairs provides any reason for optimism. On the contrary, it reminds me of the old Soviet joke about a citizen who is finally given permission to leave the U.S.S.R. and is shown a globe to select a new home for himself. Having slowly spun it around a few times, in careful consideration, he looks up and asks: "Is there some other globe I can look at?"

We don't have another globe and the one we have does not reflect the reality of geopolitical boundaries, or alliances, of superpower spheres of influence. It does not reflect the new geopolitical division of the world.

Russia's aggression against Ukraine, in February 2022, revealed a trend: the weakening of the position of democracy and the strengthening of authoritarian regimes – a phenomenon that will occupy political scientists and professors of modern history for years to come. This is the "Ukraine Factor".

Ukrainians are living within the moving walls of their reality – dealing with day-to-day issues which are manageable. At the end of the summer, we harvested our crops. The yields were poorer than in 2024 due to unexpected late spring frosts and a cool damp summer, but we still prepared for the winter as best we could and will now wait for spring.

The approach of the fourth anniversary of the beginning of the full-scale Russian aggression makes us look back and consider how Ukrainian society has changed.

The time of collective solidarity that surprised the whole world in 2022–3 has passed. The need to help each other is no longer so urgent. There is help from public organisations, from the state, from foreign donors.

The search for internal enemies is also over. Even children understand that the only real enemy of Ukraine is Russia and its current leadership. Yes, our inadequacies and, above all, our corruption, weaken the country, but civil society remains strong – still prepared to fight against these ills, often more actively than the official bodies set up to combat them.

The key discovery of this war-time year for me has been the new role of Istanbul. Not Erdogan's renewed attempts to become a peacemaker and bring Putin and Zelensky to the negotiating table – Erdogan has already more or less lost or abandoned this role. I am talking about the fact that Istanbul has become a meeting place for divided Ukrainian families. Thousands of Ukrainian refugees from all over the world regularly travel there to meet relatives who have remained in the occupied territories or ended up in Russia. Istanbul is the most accessible point on the map – easy to get to from Russia and not so difficult from the occupied territories of Ukraine. Hundreds of buses travel from Russia to Istanbul via Georgia. There are dozens of flights every day from all over Russia, 54 per week from Sochi, the city near Putin's favourite residence. Crimean Tatars whom Russia does not allow to return to the peninsula also go to Istanbul to meet their relatives from annexed Crimea.

Inside Ukraine there is another kind of migration – internally displaced people who travel to Kyiv to meet, reminisce and plan their survival. Numerous volunteer groups provide valuable support for I.D.P.s and particularly for their children. Their plight makes me feel so grateful that I can still live at home. For all of us the future remains unstable, treacherous, broken. The new geopolitical reality deprives us of any vision of the future.

A.K.

Kyiv, one week after the heaviest nighttime aerial bombardment of the city centre so far, which killed 25 people and injured 53.

Acknowledgements

"Escalation", 16.04.2024, was originally published in edited form as two articles in the *Kyiv Post* on 20.04.2024 (https://www.kyivpost.com/opinion/31352) and 28.4.2024 (https://www.kyivpost.com/opinion/31558)

"Ukrainian Bananas – a Story of Survival", 23.04.2024, was originally published in edited form in the *Kyiv Post* on 04.05.2024 (https://www.kyivpost.com/opinion/31949)

"Stories that Come to an End", 30.04.2024, was originally published in edited form in the *Kyiv Post* on 11.05.2024 (https://www.kyivpost.com/opinion/32364)

"Beautiful Views and Ugly Occupation", 27.05.2024, was originally published in edited form in the *Kyiv Post* on 02.06.2024 (https://www.kyivpost.com/opinion/33572)

"Tears at the Train Station", 12.06.2024, was originally published in edited form in the *Kyiv Post* on 15.06.2024 (https://www.kyivpost.com/opinion/34283)

"Generating Electricity and Crime", 24.06.2024, was originally published in edited form in the *Kyiv Post* on 06.07.2024 (https://www.kyivpost.com/opinion/35409)

"War Invades the Summer", 08.07.2024, was originally published in edited form in the *Kyiv Post* on 28.07.2024 (https://www.kyivpost.com/opinion/36424)

"Tuareg Rock – A Distraction from Everything Else", 30.07.2024, was originally published in edited form in the *Kyiv Post* on 04.08.2024 (https://www.kyivpost.com/post/36818)

"Return to Kursk", 13.08.2024, was originally published in edited form in the *Kyiv Post* on 15.08.2024 (https://www.kyivpost.com/opinion/37411)

"Counting on our Military Engineers", 10.09.2024, was originally published in edited form in the *Kyiv Post* on 29.09.2024 (https://www.kyivpost.com/opinion/39728)

"Public Desertion and Going Home to Die", 25.09.2024, was originally published in edited form in the *Kyiv Post* on 30.09.2024 (https://www.kyivpost.com/opinion/39793)

"War and the Psyche", 10.10.2024, was originally published in edited form in the *Kyiv Post* on 14.10.2024 (https://www.kyivpost.com/opinion/40480)

"Nuclear Dreams and Reality", 23.10.2024, was originally published in edited form in the *Kyiv Post* on 29.10.2024 (https://www.kyivpost.com/opinion/41252)

"Adding Fuel to the Fire", 07.11.2024, was originally published in edited form in the *Kyiv Post* on 10.11.2024 (https://www.kyivpost.com/opinion/41961)

"Putin and the Full Moon", 18.11.2024, was originally published in edited form in the *Kyiv Post* on 02.12.2024 (https://www.kyivpost.com/opinion/42856)

"Feeling Our Way to the End of the Year", 04.12.2024, was originally published in edited form in the *Kyiv Post* on 06.12.2024 (https://www.kyivpost.com/opinion/43404)

"Naive Art and Sobering Reality", 17.12.2024, was originally published in edited form in the *Kyiv Post* on 22.12.2024 (https://www.kyivpost.com/opinion/44240)

"Fast Away the Old Year Passes . . .", 01.01.2025, was originally published in edited form in the *Kyiv Post* on 05.01.2025 (https://www.kyivpost.com/opinion/44855)

"Two Empty Seats", 06.01.2025, was originally published in edited form in the *Kyiv Post* on 19.01.2025 (https://www.kyivpost.com/opinion/45583)

"A Tale of Two Machos", 28.01.2025, was originally published in edited form in the *Kyiv Post* on 02.02.2025 (https://www.kyivpost.com/opinion/46450)

"On a Wing and a Prayer", 15.02.2025, was originally published in *The Sunday Times* on 16.02.2025 (https://www.thetimes.com/world/russia-ukraine-war/article/trump-can-live-without-ukraines-rare-metals-we-cant-live-without-hope-sjrpq3jvk)

"The White House Reality Show", 28.02.2025, was originally published in the *Guardian* on 28.02.25 (https://www.theguardian.com/commentisfree/2025/feb/28/ukraine-us-minerals-deal)

"War and Europe", 13.03.2025, was originally published in ABC, Spain, on 03.04. 2025

"Thinking about the Future", 29.03.25, was originally published in the *Spectator* on 29.03.25 (https://www.spectator.co.uk/article/steve-witkoff-is-wrong-to-see-peace-in-putins-eyes/)

"So Much Left Unwritten" was originally published in *P.E.N. International* on 24.02.25 (https://publishingperspectives.com/2025/02/pen-international-kurkov-on-ukraines-tragic-anniversary/)

Index

A
A Diary of War and Justice
  (V. Amelina) 195–6
activists, Ukrainian 58, 92–3,
  113–14, 157–8, 183–4
advertising, online casino 9, 13–14
Agathangel, Odesa Metropolitan
  121–2
aid, international financial and
  military 64, 67, 77, 94, 97, 102,
  103–4, 147–50, 158, 167–8,
  181, 200
air raids/air raid warnings 54, 64,
  69, 108, 125, 136, 164
  see also missile and drone
    attacks on Ukraine
Airforce Capability Coalition for
  Ukraine 64
airport closures, Ukrainian 153
"Akhmat" battalion, Chechen 62
allies, international 64, 67, 94,
  95, 112
  see also Europe; N.A.T.O.; Poland;
    United Kingdom (U.K.); United
    States of America (U.S.A.)
Ameline, Victoria 71–2, 195–6
Amsterdam, Robert 18
Anti-Corruption Foundation 37
arson attacks in Kyiv, Russian
  backed 46–7, 49

art exhibitions, Kyiv 118–19, 120
Artemovsk salt 188
Astrology, Moscow Academy of 87
Avdiivka 9, 193
Averyanov, Oleg 52
Azovstal steel plant, Mariupol 40
Azoz Battalion 113

B
banana palms 21–2
Bar 13, Kyiv 55, 180
Barkhmut 155, 192
Batkivshchyna party 114
Battle of Kursk (1943) 61–2
  dismantling of Soviet frieze
    commemorating 64, 65
B.B.C. (British Broadcasting
  Corporation) 29–30
"Be Visible" project 92–3
Belarus 70, 71, 139, 167, 178
  air defence against Russian
    drones 79–80
Belgorod 19–20
Biden, Joe 16, 106, 110, 175
Bila Tserkva 164
Bilenky, Mykola 30–1
blind and visually impaired
  Ukrainians 92–3
"Bloody Sunday," Polish 137
body armour sales, Russian 20

Bogdanov, Ilya 96–7
bomb attacks, terrorist 160, 189
bomb shelters 53–4, 187
book publishing industry, Ukrainian 180
Borisova, Olga 127
Borodyanka 155
Boryspil International Airport 153
Bucha 155, 178
Budanov, General Kyrylo 36, 48, 64–6, 168
Budapest Memorandum (1994) 93, 117
"busification" 83–4
business closures, Ukrainian 25–6
business ventures, increase of Ukrainian small and medium-sized 25
Buzhansky, Max 60

C
Canada 93, 147, 151
car dealerships, Ukrainian 28
"Carol of Bells" (M. Leontovych) 92, 97
Carpathian Mountains 50
carpet-beating video, defiant and ironic viral 69–70
carpet donations for the front line 74
casinos, online 9, 11–14, 23
Cervetti, Marco 105, 187
"Champagne," Russian 73
Chapaev sweets, Soviet 65
Chasiv Yar, Ukraine 15–16
Chechen "Akhmat" battalion 62
Chechen Republic 73

Cherkasy city 49
Cherkasy region 116
Chernihiv region 62
Chernyshev, Oleksiy 116
children, Ukrainian 20, 32, 33–4, 116, 133–4, 150, 170
China 52, 109, 158–9, 175
Chorea Kozacka 136
Christmas 97, 115–16, 118, 133
　Azerbaijani plane shot down 134
　Russian anti-Christmas video 133
　trees 99, 118, 133
　underground festivities in Kharkiv city 133
churches, illegally built 16–18
circus workers 30–4
cockroaches 69–70
C.O.F.C.O. corporation, China 175
coinage, Ukrainian 76–7
Colombia 147
compensation and support for veterans' families 49, 191–2
conscription, military 26–7, 30–1, 41–4, 47–8, 82–4, 95, 114, 116, 190
construction companies, increase in Ukrainian 25
Cosmolot 13
Crimea 37, 51–3, 108, 132, 163, 169, 177–8, 200–1
criminal activity, war related civilian 46–9, 116, 160, 184–5
criminal elite, Ukrainian 116
crocodile park, Feodosia 53–4

culture, the war and destruction of Ukrainian 196–8
currency, Ukrainian 76–7
cyber-terrorist attacks, Russian 131

D
Death and the Penguin (A. Kurkov) 144
demobilisation processes, lack of 81–2, 84–6
Denmark 64, 147, 151
desertion 95
   charges of 42–4, 84–6
   lack of demobilisation processes 81–2, 84–6
   publicly announced 81–2, 84–5
Desyatynna/Tithe Church, Kyiv 17
"Diya" (Action) government system 80, 131–2
Dnipro River 10, 40, 140–6
Donbas region 15–16, 33, 37, 61, 67, 74, 89, 108, 132, 158, 163, 168, 169, 188, 189, 192
Donetsk region 92, 129–30
drivers, increase in female 26
driving test, availability 26
D.T.E.K. 49
Dyumin, Aleksey 63
Dzhelyal, Nariman 52–3, 126

E
"elections," Russian presidential 37
elections, Ukrainian presidential 189–93
electricity supplies 21, 45–6, 49, 77, 105, 126, 165

electronic defence system, Ukrainian 136–7, 139
"energy truce," Russian—Ukrainian 189
enlistment officers, Ukrainian 47–8, 82–4, 114, 116
   see also conscription; desertion; Law of Mobilisation
President Recep Tayyip 200
Europe 156, 161, 174–5, 177–8
   Ukrainians living in 26–7, 41–2, 43–4, 190
European Court of Human Rights 183–4
European energy system 126
European Solidarity party 158
European Union (EU) 103, 108, 124, 177–8
Eurovision Song Contest 29, 53
evacuations, Ukrainian 74, 129, 181
Evans, Ryan 71
"Executed Renaissance" 196–7
extortion rackets, Ukrainian 49, 120–1

F
F-16 fighter jets 64
Facebook 24–5, 53, 56, 89
fake news, Russian 150
Farion, Iryna 58–60
farming/agriculture, Ukrainian 74, 179, 199–200
Federsal Security Service (F.S.B.) 63
Feodosia 53
Festival of Ideas, Kyiv 82

Fesun, Anna 88–9
Fico, Robert 113
Finland 190
firewood supplies and laws 98–100, 101
fishing industry 35
fishing on the Dnipro River 141
food prices 115
forestry management 98–9
Forum of Amateur Circus Acts, Kyiv 33
Forum of the Russian Opposition, Lviv 36–7
France 73
Franko, Ivan 60, 75

G
Gambler magazine 13–14
gambling/gambling industry 9, 11–14, 23
Ganul, Demayn 184
Gapchinska, Dima 65
Gapchinska, Evgeniya 64–6
gas and oil supplies 21, 79, 98, 169, 174
generators, petrol-powered 45, 49
Georgia 190
"Geranium" drones, Russian 186–7
Gerasimov, General Valery 63
German Command, WWII 62
Germany 27, 93, 113
Gnezdilov, Sergiy 81–2, 75
government, Russian Federation
 ban on "magic services" 87, 91
 Budapest Memorandum (1994) 93, 117
 compensation for Kursk residents 132–3
 Federal Security Service (F.S.B.) 63
 isolationist and consumerist propaganda 127
 "presidential elections" 37
 "soft" punishment of cultural figures 52
 stance on drones over Belarus 79–80
 State Duma 63, 72, 73, 87, 91, 127
 territorial amendments to the Constitution 123–4, 127
 Ukrainian offensive in Kursk Oblast 62, 63, 66, 71
 "Zaporizhzhia Virgin Lands Resettlement" 39–40
 see also Putin, Vladimir
government, Ukrainian
 Belarusian border provocation 71
 Budapest Memorandum (1994) 93, 117
 Central Electoral Commission 192–3
 demobilisation processes 81–2, 84–5, 86
 Diya government services system 80, 131–2
 exemptions from conscription 30–1
 Forum of the Russian Opposition, Lviv 36–7
 illegal firewood laws 98

incentives for the retention of male citizens in the Ukraine 190–1
launch of the Ministry of National Unity 116–17
Law on Mobilisation 26–8, 41–4, 86
Main Intelligence Directorate 64–5
meetings with the US government 172–6, 180, 181–2
Ministry of Foreign Affairs 26
National Day of Prayer 154
national mental health issues 89
National Security and Defence Council 157–8
N.A.T.O. 94–5, 112–13, 117
passport renewals 26–7
petition against online gambling 11–13, 14, 23
pharmaceutical industry 114–15
presidential elections 158, 189–93
public handouts 115
purchase of Russian nuclear reactors 154
regulation of "esoteric services" 88
resignations and dismissals 75–6
Russian cyber-terrorist attack 131
sanctions against Ukrainian oligarchs 157–8
State Executive Services 17
support for veterans and their families 191–2
suspension of U.S.A.I.D. programmes 147–8
"Victory Plan" 90–1
see also conscription; desertion; Zelensky, President Volodymyr
graffiti, anti-Ukrainian 46
Greenland 147, 150–2
"grey passports," German issue 27
Grivko, Serhiy 88
Gurulev, General Andrei 63
Guskov, Yuri 39–40

H
haiku 57
"Hero of Ukraine" awards 23, 60
Hryb, Lieutenant Colonel Igor 90
Hrytsk, Yaroslav 138–9
human bomb terror attacks 160
Hungary 70, 95, 109, 126, 153, 179
Hydropark, Kyiv 142, 143, 144

I
illegal immigration/desertion 27, 28, 41–4, 81–6, 95
Independence Day, Ukrainian 67–8, 71
intelligence agencies, Ukrainian 64–5, 159
Internally Displaced Persons (I.D.P.s) 100, 126, 132, 170, 201
Iran 15–16, 109
Iranian drones 15, 16, 72, 77, 79, 80–1, 136
Israel 15–16
Istanbul 200
Ivano-Frankivsk 184

J

Jamala 53
Japan 57–8
journalists, RF targeting 71–2
judges, shortage of 42–3, 121
Jungle Cat café, Kyiv 143–4

K

Kadyrov, Ramzan 73–4
Kaganovska, Tetyana 72
Karandieiev, Rostyslav 30, 31
K.G.B. 72
Kharkiv city 69, 133
Kharkiv region 29–30, 33, 61, 74, 167
Kherson city 127
Kherson region 10, 37, 102, 175
Khinshtein, Alexander 133
Khmelnitsky 187
Khmelnitsky Nuclear Power Plant 19, 154
Khortytsia 143–4
Kim, Vitaly 96
Kiper, Oleg 121
Kivertsi court, Volyn region 42
Klitschko, Vitali 114
kopeck coins 76–7
Koreans, Ukrainian 96
Kornienko, Vladislav 33
Kosice train station, Slovakia 41
Kozhevnikov, Viktor 99
Kramatorsk 71, 72
Krasovytskyy, Oleksandr 180
Krivetska, Nelya 92
Krynki village, Ukraine 10–11
Kuleba, Dmytro 75–6
Kuliev, Timur 32
Kupyansk 29–30
Kursk Oblast, Russia 61–4, 66, 67, 71, 90, 96, 132–3, 168–9, 181, 192
Kvilinsky Garden, Poltava region 24–5
Kvilinsky, Jan and Olga 24–5
Kyiv
   activism supporting Ukrainian PoWs 113–14
   air raids 54, 124–5, 136, 187
   Art Mall exhibitions 136
   Bar 13 55, 180
   central children's hospital bombed 54, 125
   Christmas festivities 116, 118, 133
   Desyatynna/Tithe Church 17
   Dnipro River 140–6
   enlistment practices 83
   Festival of Ideas 82
   the "Ghost of Kyiv" 23–4
   Hydropark and Trukhaniv Island 142–3, 144, 145
   Ivan Franko Drama Theatre 136, 139
   missile and drone attacks 70, 77–8, 124–6, 135, 136–7, 139, 162, 164, 187
   Moscow Patriarchate 16–18
   naive art exhibition: "Naive Free" 118–20
   Nariman Dzhelyal dines with author 126

National Museum of the History of Ukraine in the Second World War 64–6
New Years Day drone strike 136–7, 139
opening pedestrian bridge for the city's 1,542nd birthday 40
outbreak of war (2022) 162, 167
Pan-Syo Korean restaurant arson attack 96–7
power supplies 45–6
Russian backed arson attacks 46–7, 49
State Circus 33
Kyiv-Pechersk Lavra monastery 144
Kyiv School of Public Administration 191

L
language in Ukraine, Russian 58
Latin American journalists 71–2
Latvia 80
Latyshev, Oleg 85
Lavrov, Sergei 175
Law on Mobilisation 26–8, 41–4, 86
Leontovych, Mykola 92, 97
Likhachev Cemetery 131
Lithuania 80, 178, 190
Logvinenko, Bohdan 148–9
Ludvig Nobel Prize 73
Luhansk 34
Lukashenko (aka "Cockroach"), Alexander 70, 71, 79, 178

Lviv
Forum of the Russian Opposition 36–7
Likhachev Cemetery 131
Lychakiv Cemetery 156
shelling of apartment blocks 75
State Circus 32
State University 58, 60
Lyubeshivsky district 42

M
"magic" and "esoteric" services 87, 88, 91
Maidan riots 163
Main Intelligence Directorate, Ukrainian 64–5
Mali, Africa 55–6
mannequin decoys 10–11
Mariupol 40, 113, 155, 179
Mariupol theatre 197
marriages, online 80
martial law and Ukrainian election campaigns 190–1
Maryinka 129
mass graves in Ukraine, exhumation of Polish 138, 139
McDonald's 19
medical supplies 114–15
Melitopol 38, 39
mental health in Ukraine 89–91
soldiers 90
Meshkova, Lyudmila 135
migrants, Russian 39–40
Military Chaplains Corps 24

211

missile and drone attacks on
  Ukraine 63–4, 69, 70–2, 75,
  105–6, 108–9, 111, 118, 124–6,
  128, 129, 141–2, 162–3, 164–5,
  181, 186–8, 192, 196, 197–8
Mobilisation, Law on 26–8,
  41–4, 86
monetary cost of war 77
morale and character, Ukrainian
  67–8, 69, 88, 89–91, 120–1, 122,
  128, 143, 150, 154–5, 156–7,
  165, 169–70, 180
Moriyama, Masahito 57–8
Moscow Academy of Astrology
  87
Moscow Circus 34
Moscow Patriarchate, Church of
  the 16–18, 121–2
"Mother of God" exploitation
  scandal 88–9
Mukachevo 106, 108–9
Munich Security Conference 153,
  156
murder of Demyan Ganul 184
murder of Iryna Farion 58–60,
  184, 195–6
murder of Volodymyr Vakulenko
  195
music trends 55–6, 58, 60
Musk, Elon 107
Muslims in the Russian Federation
  127
Mykolaiv city 50, 160
Mykolaiv region 50, 96

N

naive art, Ukrainian 118–20
naivety and Ukrainian character
  120–1, 122
National Bank 76
National Museum of the History
  of Ukraine in the Second World
  War 64–6
N.A.T.O. (North Atlantic Treaty
  Organization) 15, 48, 94–5, 103,
  112–13, 117, 155, 179
Navalny, Alexei 37
Nayem, Masi 84
Nazi Germany 137
Netherlands 64
New Time radio station, Kyiv
  13–14
N.G.O.s, Ukrainian 92–3, 99,
  148–9, 157, 191–2
Nobel, Ludvig 73
"Nobel Prize," Russian Federation
  73–4
Nobel, Robert 97
Noginsk, Russia 18
North Korea 95–7, 109, 125, 127
Novorossiysk port 35
nuclear arsenal and capabilities,
  Ukrainian 93–5
nuclear power plants 19, 154
nuclear weapons, Russian
  Federation 93–4, 96, 125

O

Obama, Barrack 93–4
occupied Ukrainian territories
  10–11, 15, 34, 102, 108, 111,
  168, 169–70, 171, 200

acceptance of Russian citizenship 38–9, 101
evacuations 74, 129, 181
Ministry of National Unity 116–17
Moscow Circus performances in 34
property laws and confiscation 38–9, 53, 100–1
prospect of exchange for peace 154–5
rare earth metal supplies 158–9
real-estate records 132
return of internally displaced persons (I.D.P.s) 100
Russian migrants 39–40
Russian passports 38–9
Russian "presidential elections" 37
see also Crimea; Donbas region; Kherson region; Zaporizhhia
oceanarium, Crimea 51, 53
Odesa 35–6, 50–1, 163, 165, 183, 187
Cathedral 197
oil trade, Russian 169
Olenya airfield, Russian Federation 55
oligarchs' sanctioned, Ukrainian 157–8
online casinos 9, 11–14, 23
online marriages 80
Open Society Foundation 149
Operation "Stream" 194
opinion polls, Ukrainian 169–70
Orange Revolution 163
Orban, Viktor 70, 108–9, 113, 126
Organisation of Ukrainian Nationalists 137
Orthodox Church of the Moscow Patriarchate 16–18
Orthodox Church of the Saviour on Spilled Blood, Yekaterinburg 194

P
Palamarchuk, Natalia 156
Palamarchuk, Vasyl 156
Pan-Syo Korean restaurant arson attack, Kyiv 96–7
Panama 147
Paris Olympic Games (2024) 60
passport renewal, Ukrainian 26–7
passports, Russian 38–9
peace/end of the war, the prospect of 153, 154–5, 157, 159–61, 168, 169–71, 174, 175, 181–2, 186, 189, 200
Peskov, Dmitry 71
pests, house 69–70
Petrichenko, Pavlo 11–13, 23
pharmaceutical industry, Ukrainian 114–15
"pipeline" war symbolism, Russian 193–4
Podolyak, Mikhailo 36
Pokalchuk, Larisa 100
Pokrovsk 74, 92, 129–30, 159
Poland 27, 70, 137–8, 178
Volyn tragedy (1942—43) 137–9
police force, Ukrainian 46, 48, 120–1, 183
specialised military 47–8

Poltava, military communication school 75
polygamy rights Russian Federation, Muslim 127
Ponomarev, Ilya 37, 72
Poroshenko, Petro 157
Potiy, Anatoly 20–1
power supplies, Ukraine 19, 45–6, 49, firewood, 105, 111, 126, 154, 165, 189
President's Last Love (A. Kurkov) 145
Primachenko, Maria 118, 119, 197
prisoners of war, Russian 62
prisoners of war, Ukrainian 113–14
propaganda, Russian Federation 20, 47, 51, 58, 62, 127, 133, 193
property law and confiscation, occupied territory 38–9, 53, 100–1
psychological and psychiatric services 89, 90
Putin, Vladimir 36, 62, 71, 73, 105–6, 111, 117, 125, 200
and Donald Trump 102–3, 106–8, 123–4, 151–2, 153, 156–7, 165–6, 170–1, 175, 182, 186, 193
and Elon Musk 107
invasion of Ukraine 163
"Moth" nickname 69
naming and dedicating years 167
Russian attack drones over Belarus 79–80
territorial amendments to the Constitution 124–5
use of shamans 91
and Viktor Orbán 108–9
and Volodymyr Zelensky 102–3, 107, 157, 175, 186, 192–3

R
railway services, disruption to 106
rare-earth metal supplies 158–9, 172–6, 189
real estate prices, Ukrainian 28
real-estate records, Ukrainian 131–2
Red Army, Soviet 65
refugees, Ukrainian 38, 74, 93, 117, 142, 147, 170, 178, 192
religion 16–18, 121–2, 127, 154, 194
"Right Sector" 184
Rodari, Marco 33–4
Romania 126
Rotaru, Sofia 53
Rozhny village 20–2
Russian Constitution 123–4, 127
Russian Federation
and the European Union 177–8
evacuation of Belgorod 20
funding Ukrainian teenage arson attacks 46–7, 49
holidaymakers 51–2
"magic services" 87, 91
naming and dedicating years 167
oil supplies 169
"presidential elections" in occupied Ukraine 37
propaganda 20, 47, 51, 58, 62, 127, 133, 193

Russian Orthodoxy vs Western cultural prestige 72–3
sanctions against 107, 157, 158, 177–8
Trump related economy boost 156
the U.S. and rare-earth metal supplies 173, 189
Russian Federation military forces
air defence capabilities 11, 52
annexation of Crimea 163, 177–8
attack against Avdiivka industrial zone 9
attack drones 9, 16, 63–4, 70, 72, 77–80, 105, 124–5, 135, 142–3, 164–5, 186–7
attack the Sumy region 181
attacks from Belgorod 19–20
capture of Avdiivka city 193
capture of Vuhledar 89–90
Chechen "Akhmat" battalion 62
conscription of prisoners and homeless 78
Dnipro River 10, 141–2
drone crash in Latvia 80
drones over Belarus 79–80
facilities in Crimea 51–2
fighting on the side of Ukraine 36
intercontinental ballistic missiles 111
invasion of Ukraine (2022) 162–3, 167, 199–200
Kharkiv region offensive 29–30
mannequin decoys 10–11
missile and drone attacks on Ukraine 19–20, 63–4, 69, 70–2, 75, 77–8, 105–6, 108–9, 111, 118, 124–6, 128, 129, 141–2, 162–3, 164–5, 186–8, 192, 196, 197–8
murder of surrendered Ukrainian soldiers 89
naval fleet 35, 163
at the northern border to Ukraine 181
nuclear weaponry 93–4, 96, 125
Olenya airfield 55
Operation "Stream" 194
Oreshnik warheads 125
Pokrovsk offensive 129–31, 159
precision strikes against Ukraine 71–2, 75
Russian prisoners of war 62
sea mines 50
shoot down Azerbaijani plane 134
support from North Korea 95–7, 125, 127
Ukrainian offensive in Kursk Oblast 61–4, 132, 168–9, 181, 192
Ukrainian tactical G.P.S. interference 136–7
use of underground pipelines 9, 193–4
"Russian Spring" 183
Rutte, Mark 113

S

Sadovyi, Andriy 36–7
salt supplies 188
Samar 131
sanctions against Russian Federation 107, 157, 158, 177–8
sanctions against Ukrainian oligarchs 157–8
Sapphire Hotel, Kramatorsk 71
scams and racketeering 49, 120–1
Scholz, Olaf 113
sea mines, Russian 50
Second World War 61–2, 64–5, 137–8
Servant of the People party 88, 148
Sevastopol 53–4
   beach 52, 53
shag coinage, introduction of 76
Shahed drones, Iranian 79
sharks, Russian purchase of 51, 53
Sheremetyevo Airport 38–9
Shevchenko, Taras 130–1
shipping industry 35
Shmyhal, Denys 117
shops reopening 19
Shumuk, Danilo 130–1
Sirets, Hryhoriy 42
Skovoroda, Grigory 197
Skubenko, Maxim 12
Slovakia 95, 109, 126, 178
social media
   aggression against Vitaly Portnikov 150
   destruction of Kvilinsky Garden 24–5
   introduction of new "shag" coins 76–7
   Kharkiv carpet-beater video 69
   Odesa sunrise 35
   Russian 20, 46–7, 150–1, 160
   Russian funded vandal and terror attacks 46–7
   Russian propaganda bots 47
   suspension of U.S.A.I.D. programmes 147–8, 150
   Tuareg forces 56
   Ukrainian nuclear capabilities 93, 95
   videos of Russian aggression 89–90
   vilification of circus workers 30–1, 33, 34
Society for the Blind and Visually Impaired, Vinnytsia 92
Sokur, Lesya 135
Solovyov, Vladimir 20
Sopronov, Yuriy 72
Soros, George 149
Sorosites 149
South Korea 97, 127
Soviet Union 61–2, 64, 65, 76, 115, 163, 173–4
   house pests 69–70
Soviet Victory Day 34
Special Services, Russian 150, 160, 182–3, 193
Special Services, Ukrainian 183
Spiridonov, Alexander 87, 91
Spiritual Administration of Muslims, Russia 127
State Museum of History 17

State Travelling Circus, Ukrainian 31–2
statues and monuments, Ukrainian 92, 130–1, 145, 197
Sterc-Ketch, Chechnya 73
Strana 149
Sudzha town, Kursk Oblast 61, 181, 193–4
suicide of Ukrainian battalion commander 90
Sumy region 62, 181, 192
sunrise, Odesa 35
Syrsky, General Oleksandr 86, 95

T
Tarabalka, Natalya 24
Tarabalka (aka the 'Ghost of Kyiv'), Stepan 23–4
Tartarstan 9
Tatars, Crimean 52–2, 126, 200–1
tax increases 115
teenagers, Russian recruitment of Ukrainian 46–7, 49, 184–5
Telegram 89
Terakaft 55
Tinariwen 55, 60
tourism, Ukraine 50–2, 53–4
Trade Union House fire (2014), Odesa 183–4
Transcarpathia 108–9, 126, 188
Transistria (Moldova) 177, 178
tropical fruit farm, Rozhny 20–2
Trukhaniv Island, Kyiv 142–3, 145
Trump, Donald 94, 98, 106–7, 109, 110, 123–4, 128, 161, 179, 180–1
and Elon Musk 107–8, 180
territorial ambitions 147, 151–2
Ukrainian rare-earth metals 158, 172–6
U.S.A.I.D grant suspension 147–50
and Vladimir Putin 102–3, 106–8, 123–4, 151–2, 153, 156–7, 165–6, 170–1, 175, 182, 186, 193
and Volodymyr Zelensky 102–3, 124, 157, 172–6, 180, 193
Trump, Melania 106–7
Tuareg forces 55–6
Tuareg music 55, 58, 60
Tymoshenko, Yulia 114–15

U
Ukraïner Media 148–9
Ukrainian Insurgent Army 137
Ukrainian military forces 167–8
air defence systems 63–4, 70, 125, 141, 164, 165, 186–7
conscription 26–7, 30–1, 41–4, 47–8, 82–4, 95, 114, 116, 190
control of Iranian/Russian drones 80, 164
Dnipro River 10, 141–2
drone capabilities 9, 10, 19, 35, 52, 55, 78–9, 159
F-16 fighter jets 64
the "Ghost of Kyiv" 23–4
incursion into Kursk Oblast 61–4, 66, 67, 71, 90, 95, 132, 168–9, 181, 192
Krynki village 10–11

Kyiv arson attack on military
    vehicles 46–7, 49
lack of demobilisation processes
    81–2, 84–6
mock-up/decoy equipment 11
novice training programme 95
Olenya airfield attack 55
online gambling concerns
    11–14
online reports from the front
    121
potential for a peace treaty
    159–60
prisoners of war 62, 113–14
protecting Pokrovsk 130
Russian capture of Vuhledar
    89–90
sink Russian warships 35
St Valentine's Day train rides
    160
supported by Russian battalions
    36
targeted strike at Poltava base 75
use of U.S. weapons to target
    Russian sites 110
Ukrainian Orthodox Church 18,
    121–2
Ukrainian—Polish hostility,
    historians' communiqué on
    20th century 138–9
Ukrzaliznytsia railways 160
Umerov, Rustem 86
United Kingdom
    Budapest Memorandum (1994)
        93, 117
    death of British journalist, Ryan
        Evans 71
    military forces 15–16
    support for the Ukraine 155,
        174–5
Ukrainian refugees 93
United States of America (U.S.A.)
    Budapest Memorandum (1994)
        93, 117
    and China 109–10
    government 16, 77, 91, 93–4
        (*see also* Trump, Donald)
    Iran and Israel conflict 15
    Munich Security Conference
        (2025) 156
    rare-earth metal supplies 158,
        172–6, 189
    supply Ukraine with F-16 fighter
        jets 64
    support for Ukraine 77, 102,
        103–4, 147–50, 155, 158,
        161, 179, 181
    trade tariffs 147
Ukrainian diaspora 104
Ukrainian expat support for
    the Moscow Patriarchate
    18
Ukrainian refugees 93, 200
Ukrainian use of US weapons
    64, 110
Ukrainian "Victory Plan" 91
see also Trump, Donald
uranium supplies, Ukrainian
    93–4
U.S.A.I.D. programmes, suspension
    of 147–50

V

Vakulenko, Volodymyr 195–6
Valentine's Day (2025) 156, 160
Valetov, Yan 94
Vance, J.D. 156, 173
vehicles, state seizure of private 28
Venezuela 109
"Veteran's Spouse" online support course 191–2
veterans, Ukrainian war 83, 85
village life, author's
Vinnytsia central park 92
Volkov, Alexey 180
Volyn region 42
Volyn tragedy (1942–43) 137–9
Vorozhbit, Natalia 157
Vuhledar city/town 89–90

W

Wagner Group mercenaries 55–6, 58, 71
War of Independence, Ukrainian 76
"Warmth of a Winged Soul" health and rehabilitation centre 24
White Army, Soviet 65
Witkoff, Steve 186
Wolf Moon 110
wood-burning heating systems 98
World Mental Health Day 88

X

X 157
Xi Jinping 109

Y

Yanukovych, Viktor 93–4, 115
Yugoslavia 177

Z

Zablotsky, Marian 147–8, 150
Zakarpattia, Hungary 70, 74
Zaluzhny, Valeriy 192
Zaporizhzhia 127, 143
Zaporizhzhia nuclear power plant 19
Zaporizhzhia region 33, 37, 39, 74, 102, 106, 158, 175
"Zaporizhzhia Virgin Lands Resettlement" 39–40
Zara 19
Zelensky, President Volodymyr 9, 114, 157, 163, 167, 200
  anti-gambling petition 11–13, 14, 23
  Diya government services system 131–2
  and Donald Trump 102–3, 124, 157, 158, 180, 193
  televised White House meeting 172–6, 180
  firewood laws 98
  Italian *Il Folio* newspaper interview 150
  Law on Mobilisation 26–7
  Nariman Dzhelyal made ambassador to Türkiye 126
  and N.A.T.O. 15, 94–5, 117, 124
  presidential elections 189, 192, 193

revised victory strategy 97
"Victory Plan" 90–1, 94–5
and Vladimir Putin 102–3, 107, 157, 175, 186, 192–3
"winter support" gift 115

see also government, Ukrainian; peace/end of the war, the prospect of

Zima, Igor 135
Zinchenko, Vyacheslav 60–1